SAM Somervell
White Horse
Beghill Green
Tingley
Wakefield
W. YORKS.

D1325443

Rock Climbing in Wales

Rock climbing in Wales
Ron James

Constable London

First published 1970
by Constable & Company Ltd
10 Orange Street London WC2

© copyright Ron James 1970

SBN 09 456140 1

Design: Graham Bishop & Associates

Photoset by BAS Printers Ltd., Wallop, Hampshire
and Printed by Ebenezer Baylis & Son Limited,
The Trinity Press, Worcester, and London

2nd edition revised 1975

Contents

Illustrations

Preface to first edition

This guide book is a collection of the two hundred climbs in Snowdonia and its near environs which I have found, during eighteen years of rock climbing, to be the most enjoyable on any particular cliff or in any one valley. Naturally, they are a personal choice, although I have allowed the reactions of clients and pupils, when guiding and instructing, to influence me. There are well over a thousand climbs in the area from which to select, plus as many variations, whilst new routes, of varied merit, are added by the score each year, and so those widely experienced in the area will, no doubt, have favourite routes of their own which they feel should have been included. However, I repeat, this is a personal choice and, incidentally, my enquiries whilst writing this book have convinced me that, in the case of at least 150 of the routes, no knowledgeable climber would argue their merit. Three additional factors have helped to produce this final selection. First, I felt that I could write only about routes I have climbed, and so, in all but a handful of cases, they are routes which I have led more than once (in one instance, over 300 times!). Secondly, certain routes are generally considered classic, and so some of these had to be included. Finally, a few of the routes are those of which I made the first ascent, and so my knowledge both of the route, and the reactions of others is naturally more detailed. I have tried not to let standards of difficulty enter into my selection, and, surprisingly, a fairly level distribution through the grades has emerged; one third of the climbs are of severe grade or lower, another third are of hard severe and very severe standard, and the remainder lie in the upper categories.

I hope that the book will serve a variety of users. For those whose visits to Wales are not too frequent, I have tried to provide an easy method of getting the maximum knowledge about the best climbs without the need to buy guide books to numerous areas, and I hope in this way it will serve to attract visitors from other areas. With this in mind, I have added a system of starring the routes, again completely personal, so that even a very short visit may not be at all wasted. For the more regular visitor, I hope to draw his eyes away from the most popular crags to those offering equally good climbing in other parts of the area. Also, by the many extra outlined notes about routes not included in detail, I hope to encourage the practice of the skill of route finding, and give a thrill akin to new routing. Finally, I hope that the descriptions, being very personal and uncompetitive will give, with the photographs, the pleasant winter reading which guide books used to give a few years ago.

Preface to second edition

In this edition some route standards have been altered and descriptions have been amended if holds, number of pitons or trees have changed. I have reclimbed many of the routes during the past five years and have had special opportunity to observe how women (either Barbara or my students at I.M. Marsh College of Physical Education) have tackled them. At one stage I began to believe that certain routes needed a special feminine grade but I resisted this urge, feeling that variations in height, shape and strength are things which need to be considered by all climbers when translating guide book standards into one's own particular scale of difficulty.

Helpful comment has come mainly from 'hard' climbers, particularly Pete Crew and other Padan Lake habitués. However, special thanks must go to Chris Baxter from Australia for a series of airmail letters giving a very thoughtful analysis of the routes and standards. Chris climbed many of the routes in one summer in Wales. Sadly, less feedback has been received about the routes in the less severe grades. Here opinion and information would be valuable from climbers who regularly climb at these standards.

Only one different climb has been substituted and this should present no complication to those like Bill Cox and Will Hurford who are at present working their way through the final few of the full two hundred.

Acknowledgements

Apart from a general thanks to the hundreds of climbers of all standards, friends, clients or pupils at the centre, who have shared with me the climbs described here, and indeed the many other good Welsh routes which have been squeezed out, a special thanks must go to those who have suffered during the production of this book. My colleagues here at Ogwen, Tony Mason-Hornby, K.C. Gordon, Dave Siviter and John Hesketh and also Carol Eaton, Roger Jones and others in the rescue team, and friends in the Chester Mountaineering Club all helped to make this book possible whilst Dai Rowlands, the true Welsh guide, shared many of the ascents in all conditions and so deserves my special thanks. By his splendid photographs, Ken Wilson's contribution is great, whilst Howell Evans, John Clare, John Jackson, Reg Phillips, Mike Swaine, Tony Jones, John Wilkinson, Dai Rowlands and Tony Mason-Hornby have added to the value and interest by their fine illustrations.

To W. A. Poucher go my thanks for the idea for the book and encouragement when it was most needed. Valerie Siviter did all the typing and arranging, and finally Barbara, my wife, had a hand in every page and in almost every hold, for more than half the routes have been climbed together. Without her drive, both off and on the hills, the routes would not have been finished, whilst the book would have remained an idea.

Ogwen Cottage Outdoor Pursuits Centre
February 1969.

I

Introduction

Snowdonia contains one of the finest collections of
short free rock-climbs in the world and there are
few other areas where so many routes and variations
have been worked out and such high degrees of pure
technical difficulty attained.

It is an area well served by good roads and of easy
access from the great cities of the Midlands and the
North, whilst even London is not too distant for
climbing weekends. Many excellent routes are to be
found on low lying crags, often s. facing, and so a
regular visitor is able to keep his standard throughout
the winter and so improve each year.

The climbs selected for this book lie generally on
the main cliffs of the area and are all in, or very near,
the National Park. (The Anglesey cliffs are an exception in this respect, lying 25 miles outside the Park).
In addition to the two hundred described, many
other worthwhile routes are mentioned in the crag
or route descriptions, or are shown on the photographs. Hence it is advisable to read the book as a
whole before dipping in for the odd route description.

The general layout is fairly simple, with the area
being divided around five centres, as follows: The
Ogwen Valley, The Llanberis Pass, around
Beddgelert, around Dolwyddelan and around
Holyhead Mountain. The introduction to each area
includes information about the type of climbing,
accommodation and camp-sites, equipment shops,
guiding and mountain centres, mountain rescue
facilities and any special notes. The routes are then
grouped by crags, working in a circular fashion
around each centre. Finally, any notable routes on
outlying crags and crags with only one selected route
are grouped in a final section, again in a circular
fashion. The names used give no great variance to
those used on os maps or in other guide books, but
in some cases I have clung to old familiar names for
a crag or route, rather than make impetuous changes
which seem often to require altering again a few
years later.

Crag descriptions
As in all sections of the book, I have tried to give the
maximum information in the minimum words. Hence
each crag title is followed by its orientation, average

height of base above sea level, effective height of the rock face and a six-figure grid reference referring to the centre of the foot of the face. The first few sentences describe the position of the crag and the easiest route of access. More complex approaches are not described – it is hoped that rock climbers still possess some of the skills of the mountaineer and can devise other approaches by use of the map! Finally, a walking time for an average rock climber is given.

Then follows brief remarks about parking places for cars at the nearest road side and information about mountain rescue facilities available for the cliff.

The description of the crag is brief, involving only major general features and the routes to be detailed in the text. For some crags a photograph with routes marked will be the best aid to finding the starts of climbs and tracing their lines.

Crag descriptions usually end with a general comment about the type of climbing found on the cliff, mentioning any special points concerning technique, time of year, weather, etc.

Route descriptions

The routes are described from R. to L. or L. to R. depending on a crag's shape and the direction of approach advocated. In the first line will be found the commonest name for the route or combination of routes and/or variations, then its standard, length, an evaluation of its merit by a star system, sometimes an indication of winter ascents, and very brief information about the first ascent. The first sentence gives details about the line followed and the particular merits of the climb. The start is described only with reference to the crag description and the other described routes. Pitches are outlined in the usual way with some abbreviations but an effort has been made to describe, with their length, even the walking sections. Within the description of the crags and routes and sometimes on the photographs, other climbs, sometimes of similar character or slightly less merit are mentioned in order that a climber who has done some of the routes on the cliff could use this basic information to discover these others too, hence gaining valuable route finding practice.

Left and right when used are always as found when one is facing the mountain, crag or pitch whether ascending or descending.

Standards

The question of gradings for climbs is a thorny one, with adjectival systems seeming to be a little ludicrous, but if all the grades do is to simply give a means of comparison, then the method used is seen to be less important. Hence I have stuck to an enlarged adjectival system with the continental addition of plus (+) and minus(−) to show higher or lower subdivisions as follows:

$$E = Easy$$
$$M = Moderate$$
$$D-, D, D+ = Difficult$$
$$VD-, VD, VD+ = Very Difficult$$
$$S-, S, S+ = Severe$$
$$VS-, VS, VS+ = Very Severe$$
$$HVS-, HVS, HVS+ = Hard Very Severe$$
$$ES-, ES, ES+ = Extremely Severe$$

This gives a choice of twenty categories into which to place each climb.

Route and pitch lengths

All lengths are fairly accurate, usually with an error on the large size. Always the distance is that climbed and not as the crow flies (or some more suitable simile). Scrambling and grass pitches and walks are added in as part of the route. In some cases longer pitches have been described than is usual so that the best stances and belays can be utilised.

Star system

By personal preference, general opinion, and pure popularity, routes have been awarded stars from nil to three. One can expect the three star routes to be the best in the area and so be often crowded whereas amongst those unstarred are certain classics whose charms, although present, are difficult to appreciate at the moment of ascent.

First ascents

Details of these are kept to a minimum and are intended only to give an impression of the era and, by the leaders name, the style of climb one might expect. Where many parties shared an ascent only the most typical are noted.

Winter ascents

Certain routes are marked with a **w** after the stars.

This indicates that the routes have given me good sport even under snow, with an appropriate raising of the standard. Some of the gullies gave good snow and ice climbs whilst the other routes thus marked gave practice in rock climbing on snow covered rock.

Belays, pitons, etc.
Good belays should be possible on all stances except where otherwise stated, whilst pitons mentioned are ones which seem to have become usual and permanent. Extra or missing pegs can have a large effect on the standard of a route.

Photographs
The photographs used have been, without exception, collected to give information about the climbs and the type of climbing. It is to the photographers credit, and particularly so to Ken Wilson, that many are also excellent photographs in themselves. Where possible they show the crux of a route and care has been taken to ensure that crucial running belays are visible.

Abbreviations
Abbreviations have been kept to a minimum, the principal ones used being as follows:

N. – North L. – left
S. – South R. – right
E. – East   FT. – feet
W. – West   YDS. – yards

Other guide books
The attention of readers requiring more detailed information about the other climbs in the area is drawn to the fine series of guides produced by the Climbers Club.

A The Ogwen Valley

This fine open valley runs from Bethesda to Capel
Curig and is served by the A5 trunk road. It is also
known as Nant Ffrancon. To the N. lie the Carnedds,
large rounded hills cut by long, usually uninhabited
valleys, whilst to the s. is the line of 3,000 ft. peaks
known collectively as the Glyders. Most of the big
crags lie on the far side of each Carnedd ridge facing
N. or NE and on the valley side of the Glyders, again
facing N. or NE. Small crags are found where spurs
have been truncated on each side of the valley.

The climbing in this area is best described as 'old
fashioned' giving many good routes of medium
standard. Holds generally seem good, but on the
more popular climbs are often rounded. Skill with
modern protective aids makes it not too difficult to
stay safe but on some crags the big spikes, prevalent
in Llanberis area, are absent.

The routes tend to be possible in bad weather for
the well worn rocks do not get too greasy, whilst in
winter, snow makes many of the gullies and easier
rock routes fine expeditions. The Devil's Kitchen
cliffs can give very hard problems on ice.

General Facilities

The valley provides facilities which vary from
3 star AA hotels to the crudest of bivouac caves, from
excellent restaurants to a roadside tea bar and from
elegant cocktail lounges to concrete kitchen bars,
plus the usual ancillary services.

(i) Sleeping

Hotels in Capel Curig, Bethesda and Bangor. Motel
at Tyn Y Maes.

Caravan Park at Ogwen Bank above Bethesda.

Guesthouses in Capel Curig, Tyn Y Maes, Bethesda
and Bangor.

Farms with accommodation near Capel Curig and
on both sides of the road to Ogwen and at Tyn Y
Maes.

Barns at the farms above, plus one below Ogwen
Falls.

Youth Hostels at Idwal Cottage (648603), Bryn
Hall, Bangor (Tan Y Bryn), Capel Curig and
Penmaenmawr.

Climbing huts:

North Wales MC at Tal Y Braich (699604)

Midland Association of Mountaineers at Glen Dena (668605)

London University at Caseg Ffraith (684600)

Climbers Club at Helyg (691601)

Scouts at Hafod (644603)

Chester MC at Capel Curig (717578)

Liverpool YMCA at Tyn Y Maes (635638)

JMCS at Bethesda (6266)

Camp sites at Capel Curig and Gwern Y Gof Isaf. Unofficial sites at other farms in the valley, plus high camping. Camping takes place in Cwm Idwal and below Milestone Buttress, but is not officially sanctioned.

Boulders for bivouacing in the high cwms.

Mountain centres at Capel Curig, Plas Y Brenin – CCPR, Towers – Wolverhampton LEA, at Ogwen, Ogwen Cottage – Birmingham LEA, and at Tyn Y Maes, Tai Newyddion – Royal Navy.

(*ii*) *Eating*

Besides meals for residents, the hotels also provide lunches and dinners for casual visitors, whilst the Motel provides grills. Cafes are scarce all the year, but seasonal ones open in Capel Curig and Bethesda, whilst Ormes Cafe in Bethesda is always open. In Bangor Chinese and Indian restaurants can be found as well as conventional cafes. At Ogwen Falls, a tea bar is open at weekends and holiday periods.

Food can be bought in Bethesda and at the well stocked Post Office in Capel Curig. Early closing days; Capel Curig – Wednesday, Bethesda – Wednesday, Bangor – Wednesday.

(*iii*) *Drinking*

Caernarvonshire is a dry county, and so hotels and inns are not open on Sundays for the consumption of alcoholic drinks. Some of the hotels have 'Climbers Bars', notably Cobdens, Bryn Tyrch and Tyn Y Coed in Capel Curig, whilst in Bethesda The Douglas Arms makes climbers very welcome. Licensing hours 11 AM–3 PM, 6.00–10.30 PM.

(*iv*) *Public Toilets*

These can only be found at Capel Curig, Bethesda and Bangor and are proposed at Ogwen.

(v) *Garages and Breakdown Facilities*

There are two garages in Capel Curig, one of which Hughes Bros. (Capel Curig 219) does repairs. In Bethesda there are three petrol stations, usually one of these is open until 9 PM. However, the Motel at Tyn Y Maes has petrol pumps, shielded from view for planning reasons, and will usually supply petrol at most hours. Bangor has many petrol stations, and a garage doing break-downs, Jones in the High Street (Bangor 2444).

(vi) *Buses, Taxis and Hire Cars*

The Ogwen Valley. A chauffeur driven car can be hired from Hughes Bros. in Capel Curig (219) whilst taxis are frequent at Bangor station and from the following 'phone numbers: Bethesda 428, Bangor 3565, 2710, 3595, 2011, 2659, 2223, 2085. Hire cars are available from Bangor 4173 and Penmaenmawr 3392.

Finally, for those descending the Carnedds on the other sides, taxis are available from Llanwrst 640226 and Penmaenmawr 3369, whilst quite good bus services operate along the coast and inland as far as Bethesda.

(vii) *Mountain Rescue*

The official rescue post is at Ogwen Cottage OPC. (650603), Bethesda 214, which has facilities for all types of rescue, including big crag hoisting by wire and winch, and has an associated rescue team. In all cases of rescue ensure that Police have been informed, dial 999. However help may be possible at Idwal Cottage Youth Hostel and at Plas Y Brenin in Capel Curig. For accidents on the far side of the Carnedds contact Llandudno Rescue Team, via the Police.

(viii) *Public Phone Boxes*

These can be found at Tyn Y Maes (635639), Ogwen Falls (648605) and Capel Curig (620580) and Post Offices at Capel Curig and Bethesda, and Bangor.

(ix) *Climbing Equipment*

This can be bought at Arvons in Bethesda and at Browns and Brighams in Capel Curig.

(*x*) *Mountain Guides*

Most of the guides operating in the area are members of the North Wales Association of Mountain Guides and can be booked via the Secretary, K. G. Gordon, 15, Cilfodan, Bethesda, Bangor.

Plate 1. Milestone Buttress

Tryfan. Milestone Buttress
N. Facing. 1,250 ft. above sea-level. 200–300 ft. high
G.R. 663602. Plate I.

This crag, one of the most popular beginner's cliffs
in Britain, lies a few hundred yards above the A5
road, just level with the tenth milestone from Bangor.
It can be reached either direct from this milestone by
a scramble over boulders, or, easier, by a diagonal
walk from the R., or again, for the routes on the L.
side, by a path just L. of the mountain wall. This
path also leads to the N. Ridge and the E. Face climbs.
10–15 mins. is sufficient to reach any of the climbs, and
all the paths start from stiles which should be used.

Parking on roadside laybys, and car parks.

Mountain rescue equipment and a Rescue Team
are available at Ogwen Cottage Outdoor Pursuits
Centre (GR 650603).

The cliff is in two main sections divided approx.
by a line of broken rock and vegetation which leads
upwards from about 30 yds. R. of the mountain wall,
to meet a very large block, the Central Block, high
on the crag. On the R. of this central fault lie a wide
variety of beginner's climbs running up the three
obvious ribs of clean rock, which start from the screes
on that side of the crag. On the L. of the fault, corners
and grooves can be found giving harder climbs, often
slower to dry. The first of these (Route 3) starts a
few yds. R. of the dry stone wall whilst the next is
found about 100 yds. L. of the wall where a ribbon
of slab leads up to a square overhang.

1   Pulpit Route and Ivy Chimney
*D. 320 ft. * Barlow. Miss Barlow 1911.*
This combination takes the R. edge of the Milestone,
first up pleasant juggy slabs and then by the obvious
chimney just L. of *the wet descent gully (Little Gully).*

Start at the R.-most rocks of the buttress.

1   100 ft.   One or two pitches up a slab moving L.,
then up to the R. edge until it is possible to step L. to
a stance and thread belay just below the Pulpit.
2   90 ft.   Step L. from the Pulpit onto a steep slab
and move up this until a high step R. leads to an
easier slab on which one can traverse L. to behind a
flake (nut belay if required). Step awkwardly into
the trench and follow this to easier ground and a
good belay.

Here *easy traverses carry climbers completing Rowan Route* (another grade D. climb which follows a slab, a short groove, a steep nose and then a chimney about 50 ft. L. of Pulpit), *or the Direct Route across to the lower part of Little Gully, and hence, after a short traverse equipped with large natural runners, to safety.*

However, we can ignore this and scramble up 40 ft. towards the obvious Ivy Chimney on the R. It is recognisable by the large flakes jammed at the top, but the ivy has all gone.

3   90 ft. (in two pitches).   First reach the chimney via an exposed glacis and then, more difficult, enter it. One can now climb the back (dirty) or better, get up onto an enclosed slab on the L. and so reach the depths under the jammed blocks. These can be surmounted either through the letterbox on the R. (exposed but safe and traditional) or direct (gymnastic). On the stance above it is best to take a thread belay on the wall, particularly if ones companions are heavy. From this position the usual exit is via the slab on the R. until a step L. leads to easier ground. From this final slab, or from *the gully during descent* one can examine the Little Gully Wall Climb, s., which reaches this point direct from the gully bed in one 80 ft. pitch.

2   Direct Route

D+ 250 ft. ** *Barlow. Priestly-Smith 1910.*
The best route taking the nose, quite hard in some conditions. Strength or good technique an asset.

Start at the slab 20 ft. R. of a curving layback – the Super Direct – on a terrace above a little subsidiary chimney and tree.

1   100 ft.   A thin crack splits the slab and leads via a mantel-shelf to a niche in the top corner. Swing out L. onto the slabs and follow these to a large stance with fine flake belays.

2   100 ft.   From behind the flakes one moves L. to share 40 ft. with the Ordinary Route up a corner and then a L. leg jamming crack to a niche. Here the Ordinary Route goes L. over the Garden Wall, but one continues direct up a steep crack to reach the Bivalve, under which one traverses L. (exposed, and a hand traverse for those with poor footwork). Up round the corner to a stance and thread belays on the Bivalve.

From here one could escape up R. via the Ordinary

Route or even across further R. to Rowan Route, but instead one now attacks Corner Chimney in the back L.-hand corner.

3 30 ft. Enter with difficulty, wriggle up facing R., then turn round and make two exhilarating moves up the edge.

4 20 ft. Finally, the short easy slab to the top.

3 Wall Climb – Soap Gut – Chimney Route

*S+ 210 ft. * Reade 1927/Noyce 1936/Steeple 1913.*
This combination selects the best of three fine routes up the L.-hand side of the nose.

Start 30 ft. to the R. of the dry stone wall and stile with the Wall Climb.

1 70 ft. Take the well worn wall by the most direct line until below the steep nose. Then either creep off easily round to the R. (most people do this) or climb the very steep, sharp edged crack (vs+).

To reach the main section of the route, scramble up tending L. until a move or two down allows one to walk onto the terrace below the steep corner of Soap Gut.

2 90 ft. Straight up, standing well out, for 40 ft. to a ledge, then a tricky 20 ft. with a mantel-shelf onto a stance on the L. wall, with dubious belays. Then swing excitingly out onto the R. wall and so reach the Narrows via a slanting rake. Small holds on the R. wall and awkward moves in the corner (**Plate 2**) make the Narrows the crux, but finally one reaches the easier ledges of the Milestone traverse and various stances.

Soap Gut continues direct up grass and mud but in order to complete the trio one must now swing round the rib on the R. (part of the traverse) to reach another characteristic corner, called inexplicably, Chimney Route.

3 50 ft. This looks easier than Soap Gut but in fact, after 15 ft. of bridging, a move R. via a finger hold proves most trying. This however brings one to a leg gripping crack which eases as one moves higher, until a stance just below the final little pitch of the Direct Route is reached.

4 Canopy Route

*VD – 160 ft. * Steeple, Barlow 1916*
The large area of rock to the L. of Soap Gut contains numerous climbs which intermingle, and because of

Plate 2. The 'Narrows' of Soap Gut. Chimney Route is above to the R.

the damp, grassy character of the rock, are generally unattractive. However, this route by its direct finish is the best there, and gives interesting and quite difficult climbing. The Canopy itself, a large overhang, is about 50 ft. up and obvious.

Start 60 yds. L. of Soap Gut, below Canopy.

1   70 ft. Move up easily to a mantel-shelf (hard) and then follow slabs, often greasy, to below the overhang. Swing out R., good runner, and so up to the stance above.

2   20 ft. Up a little wall, the V ledge and L. to a sheltered stance.

3   70 ft. Climb up the R. wall to reach a groove; a long reach and hard move lead to a ledge from which it is possible to escape L. It is however better, and that means harder, to continue direct.

An enjoyable descent from here follows the Oblique Trench, a groove 30 ft. R. of the last pitch of Canopy, back to the V ledge; descend pitch two of Canopy and then follow easy ledges across to behind a large flake (Postern Gate). From here it is simply one move across an open chasm up to easy ground. Standard in descent is D — .

Tryfan. East Face

E. Facing(!) 2,000 ft. above sea level. 600–900 ft. high. G.R. 665592.

This, Tryfan's other great climbing ground, lies above the Heather Terrace on the face of the mountain well seen from the A5 road near Helyg. Usually, it is reached by the path starting near the Tenth Milestone. This goes up on the L. of the mountain wall and after 700 ft. it divides, the R. branch taking the backbone of the N. Ridge, whilst a lower path on the L. leads round onto the start of the terrace. Other approaches are via paths from Glan Dena (G R 668605) and Gwern Gof Uchaf (G R 673604). The Uchaf path is particularly interesting as it passes the slabs of Little Tryfan, a good practice crag. Any way the foot of the nearest route is reached rarely in under 45 mins.

Parking is as for Milestone Buttress, and also at Gwern Gof Uchaf.

Mountain rescue facilities as for the Milestone Buttress.

The face is composed of a series of five buttresses, two lower ones on the R., and then three principal ones which terminate in the three summits of Tryfan. Five gullies outline these buttresses, and so, as one approaches up the terrace, one sees Bastow Gully, deep, with rock walls but no climbing; Nor Nor Buttress, a rambling D+; Nor Nor Gully, scree filled with three easy pitches; Green Gully Buttress which starts as a D, but leads to VD+ and s climbing, and then, at the end of this introductory section, Green Gully which is grassy and does not continue below the terrace. This is the important one to recognise as all the real climbing lies above this on the terrace.

The first of the main buttresses is North Buttress with a fine route, Grooved Arête, up its R. side and with the North Buttress Climb itself up the L. hand section. Then comes North Gully, a deep, true gully climb (D+), then the terrace steepens for a few yds. to a large pinnacle with a cairn and a shallow subsidiary gully, Little Gully, *which gives a very easy way up the face*. Next, the Central Buttress with the better climbing on its left flank, starting either side of a large grassy bay. Finally, the last real gully, South Gully, broad, with occasional little pitches, and then the steep rocks of South Buttress with the hard Munich Climb starting well up the gully.

5   The Grooved Arête

VD+ 860 ft. *** **w** *Steeple, others 1911*
This is one of the best climbs on Tryfan, containing all the joys (long rib pitches, good holds, good moves) and the faults (artificiality and occasional grass walks) of the East Face. It takes all the best climbing on the R. hand part of the North Buttress.

Start 25 ft. L. of Green Gully – letters G.A. scratched on the rock.

Section 1. The Introduction.

1   120 ft.   First climb the groove, then thrutch up L. to below a slab and climb this and easy rocks above to a stance by a larger finger of rock.

2   90 ft.   Step from the belay onto the rib on the L. and follow this until after 40 ft. one can step L. into a groove. Up this with more difficulty to reach a good stance.

3   120 ft.   Climb the little overhang on the R., then walk L. and find rock to lead to a grassy path.

Walk 100 ft. across to the R. to the foot of a long curving rib of rock leading up to the main crags

Plate 3. 'Knight's Move' slab on Grooved Arête
Plate 4. (Right) The hardest of the starts to North Buttress

18

above. This is: Section 2. The Arête Proper.

4   90 ft.   Climb the rib on the R. then on the L. to a block stance.

5   120 ft.   Move up R. round the bulge into a system of grooves. Follow these, stepping L. each time one becomes unattractive, until a final swing brings one into a grassy ledge leading up L. to below the famous Knight's Move Slab.

6   60 ft.   This is the crux and is reached by a crack above the stance. From here the cracks which make the chess-board can be seen and can be followed delicately (**Plate 3**) by a variety of combinations until a small niche stance is reached on the far side. (Various harder direct variations reach this point from below, but these provide more pain and less pleasure than the proper route.)

7   60 ft.   Above the stance a series of dark grooves can be followed but, in fact, the arête on the R. provides more enjoyable climbing.

8   100 ft.   Now climb into the great block and continue on good holds up the final black wall.

This completes the climb although routes do exist up the tower ahead, to lead to Tryfan's N. summit. *It is more usual to walk down L. until the top pitch of North Gully leads to the col between the main and N. peaks. 50 ft. of scrambling lead L. to the summit whilst descent is best straight ahead down the West Face.*

6   North Buttress by the Terrace Wall Variant

D and VD 625 ft.* Jones, Abraham, Puttrell, 1899.
This route lies up the L.-hand side of the North Buttress, starting a few ft. before North Gully. The Terrace Wall is an area of steep rock lying 450 ft. above the Heather Terrace and providing many short problems. Start up the deepest groove nearest to North Gully. Those further R. are easier but less satisfying.

1   70 ft.   Climb the corner with difficulty (**Plate 4**) and protection to a good stance.

2   60 ft.   Move R. and follow a steep scoop in the main rib until it eases.

3   60 ft.   Then climb another groove further to the R.

4   250 ft.   Scrambling to the R., then back L. (a good place to carry coils or for a first lead) until a

Plate 5. Out onto the lip on Belle View Bastion

grassy terrace is reached below the Terrace Wall.

North Buttress Ordinary Route goes diagonally up
L. towards North Gully, on very easy rocks. Then
after 100 ft. it climbs a little slab back R. and traverses
to a stance behind some large flakes. From this haven
of safety, it traverses up and down to reach the flat
Belle View Terrace. However, if pitch 1 was taken
as described and found to be not too difficult, it is
better to follow the Terrace Wall Variant.

5   75 ft.   A few ft. to the R. of North Buttress Traverse, an easy line can be seen leading up to a bulge
in the wall. Turn the bulge on the R. (good hand
holds) and so move up onto a ledge (the First Ledge).
Continue direct for 15 ft. to the Second Ledge.
Belays not obvious.

6   80 ft.   Walk R. until it is possible to get onto the
L. wall of an obvious groove (the Long Chimney),
traverse the groove at the level of a large spike (runner) and move out onto the rib on the R.; climb this
onto Bollard Slab (good runners) and climb until one
is forced delicately back into the groove. Finish up
this to join North Buttress Ordinary and so step R.
on to Belle View Terrace.

7   50 ft.   Straight up on delightfully easy rock
leads to the end of the climb, from whence one may
follow the same options as Grooved Arête.

*It is possible to descend the upper part of North Gully but
the lower section is difficult and should be avoided by following
Little Gully which breaks out of it by a ledge line and cuts
into the edge of the Central Buttress. It lies in the lower part
of the face to the s. of North Gully.*

7   Terrace Wall by the Belle View Bastion

*VS. 160 ft. ** Waller, Palmer, 1927.*

The Terrace Wall (for position see Route 6) is
covered with routes and variations of which the most
noticeable are the Long Chimney (vs) starting
from a pointing finger stone, and Central Route
(vs+) a one pitch route which cleaves the line of
overhangs to the R. However, the choicest route in
these parts is the Bastion which follows the line of
the R. hand edge of the Wall.

Start at the R. hand end of the Terrace. (**Plate 3**
was taken from here).

1   90 ft.   Deceptively easy climbing up great
blocks (good runner) for 30 ft. leads round onto the
edge. Above, grooves lead up the edge of the slab

until after 65 ft. a little ledge is reached. From here one can examine the next few ft. (the crux) or look across at the Knight's Move of Grooved Arête. When ready one can move up the slab L-wards and either swing round the corner or follow it to its end. Good stance on the Grove of Bollards.

2 70 ft. Traverse out R. on the lip of the overhang (**Plate 5**) (impressive but not hard) until back on the arête, then follow this until a cunning mantelshelf L. at 40 ft. leads to easier climbing and so direct to the Terrace.

8 The Central Buttress by the Pinnacle Ribs

*D — with one pitch VD (avoidable). 560 ft. ** Steeple, Barlow, Doughty, 1916.*

The R. hand section of the Central Buttress is taken by Crevassed Rib Climb, an uninspiring VD+ whilst North Side Route, a characterless VS rises out of the junction of North Gully and Little Gully. However, the L. part of the Buttress gives excellent climbing at around D level. Two starts lie on each side of a large grassy bay, and they join at a sharp pinnacle 300 ft. up the face.

Start 30 ft. to the R. of South Gully (Initials IPR).

1 120 ft. Climb easily up blocks to the overhang, move round it on the R. and follow the R. hand groove until it is possible to step back L. onto slabs and so up these to a stance. Then continue up the steeper slabs above.

2 250 ft. In 2 or 3 pitches. Continue up easy slabs with some quite hard variants on the L. if required to reach the great pinnacle. The other start reaches this by a 50 ft. traverse.

3 45 ft. The Yellow Slab. The crux. Start directly behind the pinnacle up the well worn edge of the slab. Tiptoe R. at 10 ft. (or jump down for a rest) until hand holds arrive in a groove R. of a flake. Up this, then easier to a stance. (This pitch can be avoided to the R.).

4 75 ft. Go up L. on curving, suspiciously flakey rock until the holds improve, the angle eases and success is nigh.

5 70 ft. Anywhere to reach scree ledges below a final tower.

Those not yet satisfied may continue up Thompson's Chimney (VD+) directly ahead, not missing the chockstone runner at the ledge, but for the easiest

finish, walk round on the R. and then scramble up
to Adam and Eve.

9   South Buttress by the Gashed Crag
VD–525 ft. ** w *Buckle, Barlow, 1902.*
The South Buttress has a rather gentle main face
containing two routes suitable for beginners, Apex
Route (D−) and on its L. Arête Climb (D); but near
South Gully the rock is steeper and more continuous
and contains two superb climbs. This one is a VD −
which can easily become much harder in bad
weather. The Munich Climb described next, is a VS
of great character and interest, both immediate and
historical.
Start. The Gash, a great roof, is obvious, 200 ft. up
the buttress and the route starts directly below it,
60 ft. to the L. of South Gully at a groove.
1   100 ft.   Climb the groove moving R. on jammed
blocks at the top.
2   80 ft.   Go straight up towards the Gash, then
step R. to a stance below a chimney.
3   30 ft.   Climb the chimney with difficulty, and
continue R. over blocks to a stance.
4   30 ft.   Traverse back to the wall and mantel-
shelf up to reach the ridge again.
5   120 ft.   Follow the broad back of the ridge
without real difficulty.
6   120 ft.   Continue up the narrower ridge on easy
rock, then two grooves lead to below the final wall.
7   45 ft.   Get into the narrow chimney with difficulty and some exposure (runner on before starting)
and follow it, easing, to the summit of s. peak.
   Descent by S. Ridge or over main peak to West Gully

10   Munich Climb
VS. 285 ft. ** w *Teufel, Sedlmeyer, Jenkins, 1936.*
This superb route lies between South Gully and Gashed
Crag, and starts half way up the gully just opposite
the level of the pinnacle on the Pinnacle Rib. It has
a record of discovering parties' weaknesses in rope work
and protection and needs a steadier leader than most
routes on this mountain. However, the holds, moves
and protection are all excellent for those willing to
search a little.
   Start at a flat grass ledge just below the level of the
Pinnacle, which can be reached either up Gashed
Crag for three pitches and then a traverse or un-

Plate 6. At the piton on the second pitch of Munich Climb

pleasantly up the gully itself, or better, by a warm-up solo up the first 120 ft. of Pinnacle Rib and then a traversing walk into the L. hand branch of the gully and a 100 ft. scramble up this until easy rocks lead out L.

1 **40 ft.** Climb the groove on the R. past two runners until a weird move R. leads into a subsidiary groove and this leads to a grassy stance. Care needed here with belays.

2 **35 ft.** Climb the rectangle of slab above, first on the L. for 20 ft. to reach a small ledge. Above is a piton for protection (**Plate 6**) which is now considered proper and the very edge of the slab is climbed to reach a cramped stance amongst perched blocks.

3 **60 ft.** From the blocks, swing onto the nose to the L. and after a short move up, traverse horizontally to reach a steep flakey crack (Teufel's). It is possible to lace this section with runners. Climb the crack on good holds and jams until a final mantel-shelf leads to a stance on a grassy rake.

4 **50 ft.** Easily up the rake and behind a large block to a wide terrace. (Escape possible to the R.)

5 **70 ft.** Take the groove behind the great block with awkward moves at 35 ft. and 55 ft. to reach a rock ledge level with the last stance of Gashed Crag.

6 **30 ft.** Swing up onto the steep wall and follow it R. to the top.

Glyder Fach. Bochlwyd Buttress

North Facing. 1,450 ft. above sea-level. 120 ft. high. G.R. 656597

This cliff lies to the L. (E.) of the stream which falls out of Cwm Bochlwyd. It is best reached via the Miner's track from Ogwen Cottage O.P.C. until level with the crag, and then by a short traverse. 20 mins. easy walk.

Cars may be parked at the car parks around Ogwen and Idwal Cottages.

Mountain rescue facilities exist at Ogwen Cottage with a rescue team available, whilst extra equipment is kept at Idwal Cottage, Y.H.

The buttress presents a square face, cut at the middle of the base by twin chimneys which join at 30 ft. to continue as a single line. To their L. is a smooth face, which further L. becomes easier angled

and slightly more broken, whilst to the R. faint lines
of weakness can be seen until the much more broken
R. edge is reached.

The routes generally are short but interesting, ideal
for short days, or as an approach to Glyder Fach
Main Cliff, and those selected are characteristic of
the other routes which cover the crag. Chimney
Climb, the classic of the crag, is quite hard for its
standard, and, whilst Arête and Slab is the easiest
line on the crag, with the alternative start described
it gives delightful climbing of a good standard.

11   Chimney Climb

*VD. 110 ft. * Kirkus, Frost, 1935.*
This route takes the central weakness.

Start at the R.-hand chimney, or the arête on its L.

1   30 ft.   Climb up the chimney until it is possible
to swing out L., or reach this point via the arête.
Continue on good holds and belay on a chockstone
at the base of the chimney above and to the L.

2   35 ft.   Step L. into the chimney and move up to
the overhang (runner). Lean out on undercut holds
and with an energetic swing, move up into the
chimney above and so after a few more ft. to a poor
stance.

3   45 ft.   Continue up the chimney until, after once
again moving L., easier rock leads to the top.

On the walls to the R. of this route, at least two
routes can be found; Two Pitch, an s− which keeps
20 ft. R. of Chimney Climb, and Five Pitch, an s
which lies 20 ft. further R.

12   Arête and Slab Climb with the Marble Slab Start

*D or S+ 110 ft. or 125 ft. * Palmer, MacDonald
1927/Kirkus 1935.*
This route follows first the R. edge of the buttress, then
moves left to climb the final slab. Its variation start
reaches the first ledge from directly below.

Start. Either at the foot of the arête by a crack, or
20 ft. L., to the L. of a large bollard.

1   45 ft.   D. Climb the steep crack on excellent handholds until a scramble leads up L. to a stance.

or 60 ft.   s+ Climb the groove to the top of the
bollard, then step up L. to good spike runners below
a little bulge. Over the bulge (**Plate 7**) and then
up past a second runner to stand awkwardly on poor

incut footholds (chock runner). Now the hard move goes delicately up R. on side pulls to reach better holds and then the stance of the other start.

2   25 ft.   Step low round to the L. onto a traverse line and follow this L. for 15 ft. until an awkward move lands one on a sloping ledge. Step R. for belays.

3   40 ft.   Move back L. to make a hard mantelshelf onto the slab and follow this to the top.

13   Bochlwyd Eliminate

*HVS. 110 ft. * James, Barber, 1962.*

This climb takes a varied line up the smooth wall to the L. of the chimney. It is separated from the chimney by The Wrack (HVS) which climbs the obvious overhanging groove, and is crossed in its early part by Wall Climb, a good s which continues up a weakness to its L.

Start at the very foot of the buttress by a dirty quartz slab leading up L.

1   110 ft.   Easily up the slab until it is possible to step R. onto the rib. Up it to reach the traversing ledge of Wall Climb, and continue by a little open groove. A rounded hand traverse leads R. to a ledge. Move up to a jammed block above (runner) then either straight on, or step down R. to reach a line of holds leading up and L. with good pockets, and so to easier rock and the top.

Glyder Fach. Main Cliff

N. Facing. 2,500 ft. above sea level. 200–400 ft. high. G.R. 656587.

This fine cliff of good rough rock, rather reminiscent of Chamonix granite, lies in Cwm Bochlwyd, high on the slopes of Glyder Fach. Use the Miner's track to Bochlwyd, walk round its shores and then various paths lead up the screes to the cliff. 50 mins. walk.

Parking and Mountain Rescue facilities as for Bochlwyd Buttress.

The cliff is in three parts. To the centre and lowest is a smooth triangular slab, the Alphabet Slab. On the L. and above the apex of this is *a broken gully, the Main Gully, the usual means of descent*, whilst to its R. is East Gully, a s+ in its lower part. To the L. of Main Gully lies the East Buttress, which appears to be composed mainly of columns, and to the R. of East Gully lies the West Buttress which is smaller and

Plate 7. Marble Slab start. Over the bulge

more broken.

It is usual to approach the two upper crags by climbing the Alphabet Slab, and, whilst most of the better routes are on the E. cliff, the trilogy described on the W. gives excellent climbing at various standards. The climbing varies from the delicacy of the slabs to the hand jamming techniques of the harder routes.

14 Gamma

*S — 155 ft. * Kirkus, MacPhee, 1936.*
This climb takes a central line up the triangular slab. The only real feature on this slab is a diagonal chimney-groove which gives the rather unpleasant climbing of Beta (D—). Alpha (VS) follows the slabs to the L. of this whilst Delta (VD) lies on the R. of Gamma.

Start at the foot of the chimney-groove on a minor terrace.

1   45 ft.   After a move on Beta, step R. onto the slab and after a short (5 ft.) traverse, go up an open groove for 20 ft. (crux) until a step R. is possible. Move up a little, then traverse horizontally L. to a poor stance with good belays on the edge of Beta.

2   80 ft.   Step from the belays L. into a fine crack and go up this to easier ground and a little bay. Indeterminate climbing, as direct as possible leads upwards to a final wall. (The main problem is avoiding the easier line of Delta). Poor belay below this wall.

3   30 ft. (but **50 ft.** to a belay).   Step L. onto the wall and move up on spaced small holds to finish from a V scoop with a tricky step. Belay well back.

One is now on a terrace just below the foot of Main Gully. Scratches up the wall directly above the belay spike are Main Gully Ridge (D— but with some avoidable awkward cracks half way up). However, to the L. of Main Gully one can see the East Buttress. The next climb, the Chasm, can be seen as a line of chimneys directly to the L. of the Gully. Other landmarks are the Capstan, a large bollard 40 yds. to our L. and a little higher, and the Luncheon Stone 50 yds. horizontally L. The West Buttress can be reached from here by a traversing path to the R.

15 Chasm Route

*VD. 265 ft. ** W Thompson, Jones, Noon, 1910.*
This is an excellent climb in all conditions, which,

although escapable, feels quite serious once started.

Start directly below the line of chimneys at a series of rocky steps, 10 yds. to the R. of the Capstan.

1 50 ft. Up the rocky steps to spike belays.

2 50 ft. Continue up a cracked wall until a steep wall ahead forces one easily R. to the bed of the Chasm; up this for 20 ft. to a good belay and the real start.

3 40 ft. Up the bed to some jammed blocks, then take to the R. wall and exit between the blocks.

4 60 ft. After an initial crack, take to the L. wall and move diagonally up towards flakes on the skyline. Go behind these and then continue R. up a crack back into the gully.

5 45 ft. This pitch incorporates the famous Vertical Vice, the crux of the route, so prudence and some protection would be advisable. First climb a crack in the L. corner, then get up into a chimney-cave out of which one can step into the Vice, a strenuous L. leg jamming crack, which powerful climbers will prefer to leave as early as possible. Much time can be spent here but there is an easy way round on the R.

6 20 ft. An awkward little zig-zag crack on the L.

If one anticipates that the Vice will be too easy, a hard finish can be had by leaving pitch 4 after 20 ft. and moving R. onto the prominent rib (Chasm Rib, s) which is followed by a mantel-shelf, cracks and a chimney to its end. (This point gives excellent views of struggles in the Vice!)

16 Lot's Wife and Lot's Groove

VS. 105 ft./HVS. 110 ft. ** *Kirkus, Robinson, 1931/ 1931/Kirkus, Hicks, 1929.*

These excellent routes follow the cracks and grooves immediately L. of pitch 3 of Chasm Route and are best reached by this route or by a traverse from the gully for the impatient.

Start at the top of pitch 2 of Chasm Route; the start of the Chasm proper or even a little lower.

1 35 ft. It is usual to traverse across L. below the main groove (Lot's Groove) to reach a little corner with pocketed walls (or the purist will reach this point from below, over a little overhang). This corner is the crux and is quite testing. At the 'moment of truth' swing out L. onto the rib and up this to a resting place. Step L. again into a crack and up this to a small stance.

2   50 ft.   Awkward jamming and bridging lead to better holds and a good runner at 25 ft. Then the R. hand crack and slabs bring one to a large recess.

3   20 ft.   A slanting crack leads to a large ledge.

Lot's Groove takes the main groove direct. This is a magnificent climb which gives a delightful technical exercise. Some years ago it was reputed to have only minimal protection, but now, with the aid of nuts, etc. it can be made quite safe.

Start as for Lot's Wife.

1   90 ft.   Step L. into the groove and climb it for 40 ft. on good jams and small foot holds. Next, it is necessary to leave the protection of the corner and move up R. onto the very edge of the Chasm for a few ft. Soon one can step back into the groove and relax at a large thread runner on the L. wall, and then bridge up to the overhang. This is best climbed by backing up using a crack well out on the L. wall for the feet (Kirkus hand jammed it!) until it is once again possible to bridge. Two moves on the wall above the roof lead to good holds and a good stance.

2   20 ft.   Easily up the crack on the R. to the same ledge as the Wife.

This ledge is called the Verandah from which there are a variety of escapes. *However, if one wishes to descend then go R. to discover the flakes of pitch 4 of Chasm Route and so descend this climb for a pitch or so.*

17   The Direct Route

S– but S+ for a short section. 305 ft. ******* **w** *Ward, Gibson,* 1907.

As described here, this gives an excellent route of fairly continuous difficulty using the variations known as the Rectangular Excursion and the Winter Finish. Gibson's Chimney raises it to VS whilst the other finishes give a range of difficulty from S to HVS, although mostly only problems. Its general line is above the Capstan, climbing the rock to the left of the smooth wall which is L. of Lot's Wife. The description 'old-fashioned' is applied often to this route but one usually finds the techniques involved to be quite modern! It provides excellent sport for 'hard men' in winter conditions when some aid may be needed on the Hand Traverse.

Start at the Capstan just to the left of a rib.

1   85 ft.   Move up until it is possible to cross the rib. A little higher, recross and go up L. to a small

ledge. Climb a crack above this until it is possible
to swing R. onto the face. Move back up and from
an excellent runner (the last of many) make a long
stride R. to reach a bulging corner. Up this to a good
grass stance.

2   25 ft.   Step behind the great bollard and then
easily up R. to another sheltered stance.

3   50 ft.   Move up the groove (often greasy) on the
L. for 6 ft. then step L. and go up for 15 ft. on ledges
to some great runners. (Gibson's Chimney goes
straight up from here, backing up facing Tryfan).
Now step L., then down to the very edge of the
buttress and so toe traverse onto a jammed block in a
gully (Arch Chimney s+). Belays well to the L.

4   40 ft.   Now go back awkwardly R. to reach a large
flat ledge. Move up a few ft. to reach the Hand Traverse (crux) and a pitch needing some care. First find
a thread runner, then either hand traverse (very
strenuous) or semi-hand traverse with the L. foot also
hooked in the crack as an anchor (**Plate 8**) (ungainly
but usual) or mantel-shelf onto the crack and foot
traverse it (bold but not too difficult, although farther
to fall). All this leads to a good stance and a junction
with Gibson's Chimney.

5   35 ft.   Up by various short cracks until at 25 ft.
a large grass ledge appears on the R. (this is the
Verandah), however, continue for 10 ft. to a stance.

6   70 ft.   Walk L. along a broad flake then up the
corner crack with thread runners to the top.

*The descent gully is well to the R. and is reached by a
short scramble up and then across*, but it is better to continue to the summit, about 15 mins. scramble straight
ahead, although no doubt those who use special foot-
wear for this route will find this ending unattractive.

From the Verandah, four other finishes are possible.
They are, from L. to R., two strenuous cracks up either
side of the Final Flake (vs+ and hvs−), Hodgkin's
Variation (s+) which gives elegant climbing from
the R. hand corner of the ledge, and lastly, just around
the corner, the Final Crack (vs−) which is reached
up the Coffin Chimney. This last variant is the best,
giving an awkward problem (wrist watches should
not be worn for this pitch).

18   Slab Climb by the Spiral Variant
*D. 235 ft. * Ward, Gibson, 1907.*
The best route for novices on this section of the cliff.

Plate 8. *The hand traverse on the Direct Route*

It climbs the easier rock to the left of the Direct Route.

Start at the Capstan.

1   50 ft.   Climb a rib for 10 ft. and then traverse L. towards a chimney leading up to twin pinnacles.

2   30 ft.   Traverse L. again and make an awkward step into the chimney. Climb this and exit L.

3   30 ft.   Up a little, then up the R. hand crack, which is quite hard and so to a stance.

The direct way (VD+) reaches here from 30 ft. up pitch 1 by a diagonal ramp of slab with a very difficult narrow section near the top.

4   40 ft.   Traverse R. and then up mossy slabs to the Arch and a junction with the Direct Route just before its Hand Traverse.

5   45 ft.   Up in the L. hand corner, then, via gigantic spike holds, out onto the rib and an exposed stance.

6.   40 ft.   Delicately up the rib to its end.

The way off is to the R. scrambling upwards until it is possible to descend into Main Gully.

19   Oblique Buttress

*S. 205 ft. ** Holland, Richards, 1918.*
This route climbs the L. hand side of the East Buttress. Square Chimney Buttress (s) to its L. is equally enjoyable and gives excellent climbing. Our route lies up the clean cut buttress which starts at the lowest rocks, about 40 yds. L. of the Luncheon Stone.

Start at the foot of the rocks. The first problem is a steep diagonal crack.

1   75 ft.   Up a slab and then the R. side of a rib to grass below the crack.

2   40 ft.   Climb the crack, difficult, and so to a pinnacle. Stance to the R.

3   90 ft.   From the top of the pinnacle move onto the face and go up without difficulty to a ledge. Traverse L. and then climb straight up a rib until an awkward, out-of-balance mantel-shelf (the crux) leads R. to the top.

Descend as for other routes on this buttress.

20   Hawk's Nest Buttress

*S. 185 ft. * Abraham Bros., Thompson, 1905.*
This excellent climb, and the next route, is on the West Buttress, climbing a clean, sharp pillar of rock which lies about 150 ft. R. of East Gully and

which is dominated by the Shark Pinnacle. It is reached by an up-and-down traverse from the top of the Alphabet Slab, and follows a line diagonally R. from below the knife-edged arête to reach easier ground on the R. of the face via an obvious niche. Hawk's Nest Arête takes the challenge of the arête by a fairly direct line, whilst the Needle's Eye Climb (VD−) outflanks most of the difficulties on the R.

Start below the arête on the terrace.

1 55 ft. At first easily to a grass ledge, then R. by slabs to a flake belay.

2 50 ft. Climb up on the R. to a small ledge then on to the niche. Above and on the R. lies the mantelshelf which is the crux of the route. Reaching it is awkward, whilst standing upon it is decidedly hard. Another hard step above leads to a nook with good belays.

3 80 ft. Easily up to the R. and finally a difficult chimney in the R. hand corner, followed by an easy slab to the Shark Pinnacle.

Descend either well over to the R. (W.) or better, by the Needle's Eye Climb which takes a much easier line (VD−) up the R. hand side of the buttress using slabs, chimneys and cracks until it traverses in behind the flake.

21 Hawk's Nest Arête

*VS+ 120 ft. * Nock, Harrison, 1940.*
Hard climbing in exposed situations on superb holds. Start at the L. end of the terrace, 20 ft. L. of Hawk's Nest Buttress.

1 90 ft. Delightfully up the edge until a move L. brings one onto a large block at 40 ft. Move up the arête with difficulty, or with long arms, to reach a good hold and use this to get onto a ledge. Toe traverse a few ft. R. to a cracked corner. Up this a little until a swing out L. is possible and a wall climbed to the stance above.

2 30 ft. An easier crack to the top.

Cwm Idwal. Gribin Facet (Clogwyn Y Tarw)

N. Facing. 1,450 ft. above sea-level. 100–200 ft. high. G.R. 649596

This little cliff, which in recent years has known a variety of names, lies above the path from Ogwen to Cwm Idwal, and can easily be reached from this in a few mins. The routes are usually short, being

Plate 9. Slab climb on Gribin Facet Clogwyn Y Bustach

reminiscent of outcrop climbing, yet give such wide variety of problems as to be of value. Damp increases the difficulty considerably.

Parking and rescue facilities as for Bochlwyd Buttress.

The Gribin is a long, broken cliff which may be regarded as being in four parts. On the L., an area of broken little walls, up which Home Climb (s) starts from a tree, giving a collection of hard boulder problems. Then a big, steep wall which has been climbed direct (The Great Wall H V S) and by each of its weaknesses to the R. of this. This wall is bordered on its R. by a system of slabs offering easier climbing, and all starting from a terrace of large stones etc. *An easy descent reaches this terrace from the R., down broken ground, but this is a place for care with parties of novices.* Next comes an area of great blocks cut by deep cracks, the real meat of the cliff, with Monolith Crack finding a tunnel up the middle of these. Now the crag becomes smaller again, with great blocks lying across the path (Zig Zag starts near here) until broken chimneys and a spring merge into a tree filled gully (Wooded Gully). *This provides another descent line*, or a good route by which to introduce nervous beginners to the sport. Finally the crag drops lower, a fence comes up from the Idwal Gate, and short steep cracks cleave smooth walls.

Note: In recent years rescue teams have been called regularly to unjam knees from the cracks on this crag, particularly on Slab Intermediate and Flake Crack.

22 Slab Route by the Intermediate Start
VD − /D. 160 ft.
This makes the best of the conglomeration of ways up the area of easy slab to the L. of the central break. It takes a little corner (the start of Slab Intermediate VD −) a few ft. to the L. of the base and then continues by the clean cracked slab up the L. edge. The R. hand half of the slabs is climbed by Slab Recess Route (D −) up a series of deep cracks whilst another route exists to the R. of this, below the R. walls. These walls also give various problems, some of which can be climbed by artificial means.

Start. 10 ft. down from the flat boulders below the slabs, near a small steep corner.

I **45 ft.** Reach the corner from the R. and climb it

with difficulty to a good stance on the L. and possibly a thread belay.

2   25 ft.   Step L. onto a cracked slab and up this L.-wards to a grass ledge. Walk back to find a belay. (Slab Intermediate takes the deep crack on the R. and then the corner and slabs above).

3   50 ft.   Up the slab by zig-zag cracks to a fine flake (runner) (**Plate 9**). Step off this onto the slab above and in a few ft. to a stance.

4   40 ft.   Up L. around a corner (exposed) then either straight up over blocks or more easily R. to the top.

23   Monolith Crack

S — 160 ft. Abraham Bros. 1905.

At the lowest point of the central section of the crag, large blocks lie in profusion, whilst one gigantic monolith has slipped down a little but not yet fallen over. Around it and under it lie the starts to this famous route, at one time described as the hardest in the area. It has pleasures which are not easy to appreciate at the time!

Start just to the R. of the large block at a cave.

1   30 ft.   Wriggle up under the block to reach a stance which could have been reached by a walk from the L.

2   40 ft.   A wedge shaped block has remained in the corner above and one can reach its top by either side, both hard.

3   50 ft.   Again a choice of ways is possible. Slim leaders and masochists will dive into the depths of the main crack and struggle up past the chockstone to regain the surface. The rest will swing out R. as did M. de Selicourt and climb cracks and mantel-shelves around the corner to reach the same place (s—).

4   40 ft.   After an easy slab, a chimney leads to the top.

50 ft. to the L. of Monolith Crack lies Angular Chimney (V D), a much more enjoyable way of reaching the same point. It takes the obvious steep corner.

24   Zig-Zag

*S + 140 ft. * Herford, others, 1912.*

This possibly is the best route on the cliff. Steep and open and on good rock. It is quite hard and care is needed to protect the V-chimney adequately.

Start about 15 yds. R. of Monolith Crack on a large boulder which blocks the path.

1 80 ft. Climb up the little corner to the overhang and then swing across L. and up into a crack which leads to a sloping ledge. Cross the ledge to a low runner, stand on this and so climb up an open v-chimney (the crux) by facing R. to reach a quartz slab. Up this a little to good belays or a tree.

2 30 ft. Traverse across L. to below twin cracks.

3 30 ft. Climb either crack, the R. hand one being of the correct standard for this route. (The L. hand crack is hard, at least s+).

To the R. of this route the crag gets more broken, yielding two easier routes, Gully and Slab (D) and Seniors' Climb (D) before the Wooded Gully.

25 Flake Crack

*VS— 90 ft. * Thornycroft, 1909.*

This fine climb and a harder neighbour lie on the far R. section of the cliff, just before the fence meets it. They start from a small rocky terrace a few ft. up, easily reached from below Wooded Gully by a traverse. The climb is hard and exciting for the flake can be made to wobble, although it has stood the test of time. Wear, and the loss of a tree has increased the standard of the lower part of the route.

Start from the crevasse behind the large block directly below the flake.

1 45 ft. From the small overhung corner, get up onto the slab on the R. and from this reach a higher slab with a holly tree. Step back L. towards the crack on the R. of the flake. A difficult thread runner protects the move into this crack which is climbed facing R. until the stance behind the flake is reached.

2 45 ft. Work up behind the flake until it is possible to stand on it. One could place a runner on its tip before standing on this, and then move across onto a thin slab which soon leads to a stance.

(It is possible to climb the crack to the L. behind the flake. v s).

A nice vs, Née Langley, climbs the crack in the wall a few ft. L. of the flake, taking a stance in an old tree.

Cwm Idwal. The Nameless Cwm

Generally N. Facing. 1,750–2,900 ft. above sea-level. 200–400 ft. high.

Unlike the other routes in this section, these are not grouped as lying on one cliff, but instead, are selected because they lie in one small cwm. The Nameless Cwm, or Cwm Cneifion, lies high on Glyder Fawr bounded by the Gribin and Seniors ridges, and contains much rock, although little of note to the rock climbers. However, within this generally scrambling or winter climbing area lie three good routes. The first, leading up into the cwm is Sub-Cneifion Rib, a steep rib of rock lying midway between the Gribin Facet and Idwal Slabs. Then, at the entrance to the cwm itself lies Cneifion Arête, a delightful ridge high on the L. which leads up to the 'football pitch' of the Gribin Ridge. Finally, at the R. hand head of the cwm lies Clogwyn Du Ymhen y Glyder (often known as Clogwyn Du), a large cliff which contains the excellent Manx Wall which finishes very near the summit of Glyder Fawr. It is worth noting here that the head of this cwm and the gullies around Clogwyn Du are all excellent winter climbs often with cornices to add to the pleasure.

Sub Cneifion Rib is 400 ft. above Lake Idwal, and offers the best approach to the cwm. Otherwise, take the gully on its L. to a few ft. above its top, and then follow an excellent traversing path to the bed of the lower cwm. The screes on the L. lead to the Arête, and those ahead lead up to the foot of Manx Wall. Times vary from about 25 mins. to the Rib to over an hr. to Manx Wall.

Parking and rescue facilities as for Bochlwyd Buttress.

26 Sub-Cneifion Rib

*VD+ 300 ft. * Edwards, 1931.*

This is the clean rib of rock which lies on the hillside below the entrance to the cwm (GR 648593). It proves a delightful route, particularly for an evening climb or to follow a route on the Slabs, or as an introduction to the cwm above.

Start. 50 ft. up to the L. of the foot of the rib, between a large block and the rib itself.

1 35 ft. Step out onto the rib and go up to a crack, step L. and continue on good holds to a stance on the L.

2 40 ft. Step R. and go up a groove to a bulge.

Turn this on the L. then step back R. Next up an open groove, quite difficult when greasy, to easier rock and a stance.

Now scramble up L. for 40 ft. to the foot on the next rib.

3   80 ft.   Climb the crest of the rib by a series of little problems, culminating in a smooth slab. Belay well back.

Scramble down from the belay and round a rib on the R., and then go up to a stance on blocks below a nose.

4   105 ft.   Mantel-shelf onto the nose and traverse R. round the corner to reach a cracked slab. Up this to the crest of the ridge and then by a crack continue to reach easier climbing up more cracks to a stance. An exciting pitch.

5   40 ft.   Easily up the final crack to the top.

27   Cneifion Arête

D− 410 ft. * **w** *Barlow, Miss Barlow, 1905.*
A very pleasant route offering a feeling of an alpine ridge and giving good practice at this type of climbing, with a little difficulty being followed by 'moving together' sections. Delightful in winter or as part of a mountain day. The route climbs the slabby arête which starts about 200 ft. up the screes, just above the traversing path as it reaches the floor of the lower cwm (GR 648587).

Start just R. of the foot of the ridge.

1   70 ft.   Steep climbing on excellent holds for 30 ft., then move a few ft. R. and go straight up to the crest.

2   25 ft.   Traverse L. to reach a little chimney. Up this to easier ground.

Now continue up on the L., getting onto the jagged crest wherever possible. Some sections need belays which can be found in profusion. After about 150 ft. an awkward move from one pinnacle up onto the next, followed by slabs, getting easier to the top, although often quite exposed on the edge.

28   Manx Wall

S+ 180 ft. ** *Lowe, others, 1942.*
This tremendous route on Clogwyn Du (GR 646583) is one of the great routes of Wales and its inaccessibility adds to its attraction. It is very exposed and the climbing is excellent. An obvious gully runs up to

Plate 10. Idwal Slabs, starts of Ordinary Route and Charity

44

bound the crag on the R. (Clogwyn Du Gully, hard in winter) and closer examination reveals that the L. wall of this gully is in fact a pillar. The route goes a little way up the L. of this and then breaks out L. across the steep face and finishes directly to the top of the crag.

Start at the foot of the chimney which forms the L. hand side of the pillar, about 150 ft. up a rake.

1 45 ft.   Follow a line of weakness out L. to a stance and belays.

2 35 ft.   Get into a groove on the R. and follow it on good but small holds to a ledge. Stance and belays on the L.

3 35 ft.   Climb up above the belay then L. on a narrow grass ledge. Thread belay.

4 65 ft.   Climb the slab above (delicate) to the top of a crack, then traverse L. under the rooves. Turn these on the L. with good holds on the wall above. Finish by a steep crack.

Cwm Idwal. Idwal Slabs and Walls
N. Facing. 1,500 ft. above sea-level. Slabs 450 ft. Walls 200 ft. G.R. 645589

This great climbing ground lies at the far end of Llyn Idwal and presents a wide variety of routes of all standards, including some of the hardest pitches in the area. It can be reached up the Idwal Path in about 20 mins. from Ogwen.

Parking as for Bochlwyd Buttress.

Mountain rescue facilities at Ogwen. In the event of an accident on the Slabs, it is important that exact information be given concerning the position of the patient, for the methods of rescue and equipment required vary considerably from route to route and even by the pitch.

The crag itself can be looked upon as having four facets, although each is inter-related and each is utilized often by the approaches or escapes of one of the others. The main section is obviously the great area of overlapping slabs up which go the best known routes. Above this lies the steep rocks of Holly Tree Wall, the steep cracks and hard mantel-shelves giving complete contrast. Again, the East Wall provides delightful climbing on small pocket holds with only the occasional weaknesses and grassy ledges, and yet contains one route of superb delicacy.

Generally climbers tend to treat the Slabs as an outcrop, and so they can be on a fine summers day in rubbers, but 'benightments' are frequent, and accidents too, once conditions are not perfect. It is at this time that one realises that the Idwal Slabs and Walls are part of a big cliff and not a minor training ground.

29 The Ordinary Route

D. 450 ft. * **w** *Rose, Moss, 1897.*
Of the five good routes which climb the Slabs, this is the easiest, provided the corrected line is taken. It follows the obvious trench, 30 ft. in from the L. edge and gives less exposed climbing than the others. A good route for muscular beginners but care is needed to get the best belays.

Start at the foot of the trench (**Plate 10**).

1   150 ft.   Straight up the crack past a good spike at 50 ft. and another at 75 ft. to reach a good stance in a square niche. Low rock belay on the L., or big nut belay on the R.

2   150 ft.   Start up the rib on the R. for 20 ft., then step up and traverse horizontally L. to reach the other groove. Step L. out of this for a few ft. then back in and by a crack to a scoop (75 ft., flake belay on the L.). Move up the scoop and then out R. onto slabs with incut holds and so up easier rock to reach a good, rounded spike belay.

3   80 ft.   From above the belay, follow a rounded crack until the rock ahead steepens. Move across R. on good holds, then directly up a crack above (crux) until it eases at a good stance.

4   70 ft.   Easily up L. over large ledges, then back R. to the terrace with a great perched block.

It is possible to finish direct to the block. This is VD and is a more fitting finish to Charity than the Ordinary Route.

From the terrace, no suitable continuation up the steep walls above is possible, and so those following this route would be well advised to follow the usual way off, as indeed would those who find the other slab routes at all difficult. *This exposed way off scrambles up for nearly 200 ft. to the L. of this wall until over a bulge a path leads towards a gully and after 40 ft. more of climbing, the climber may relax and scramble down steep rocks below the wall, or better, follow a diagonal path towards Idwal Gate until a grassy traverse leads easily to the foot of the Slabs.*

Plate 11. The Twin Cracks of Hope

30 Hope

VD 450 ft. *** Mrs. Daniell, Others, 1915.

Of the three Virtues which climb the layers of slab to the R. of the Ordinary Route, this is the best route. Excellent climbing on good holds in good situations make it an enjoyable day's sport. Charity (VD), to its L. lies only 20 ft. to the R. of the Ordinary Route and, when taken by its correct start, gives a climb with an excessively difficult first 40 ft. (VD+), followed by easier and more repetitive climbing. Similarly, Faith (VD−), 120 ft. to the R. of Hope, is generally uninspired technically except in its penultimate pitch, where a rib (the Cat Walk) gives a short section of exciting climbing. 150 ft. of rope is best on these routes in order to reach adequate belays.

Start about 70 ft. to the R. of the Ordinary Route at a broken corner, below a flat ledge at 30 ft.

1   140 ft.   Up the edge of the corner to the flat ledge (belay above its R. end). Now climb diagonally R. to get onto the large slab above at its bottom R. hand corner. Keep moving across L. then up, to join together a series of good holds and small ledges, until a patch of quartz leads to a larger ledge on the L. edge. Up a small corner to a large ledge and good belay.

2   100 ft.   Above the belay lic twin cracks, the crux. They are best climbed using the R. one for the feet until a good hold is reached high up for the R. hand (*Plate* **11**). From their top, one step R. and then two long steps L. lead past spikes to a thin crack going straight up the slab. Climb this and the slab around it to reach better holds and pockets, and so reach a V-ledge just beside an overhang. Continue in the corner for 10 ft. to find a hidden thread belay.

3   150 ft.   Step L. onto the slab and then go back into the groove above. (Belay after 10 ft.). Follow this groove to a bulge, step L. and then back R. to overcome this. Then either go up R. to a stance at the top of Faith Cat Walk (hidden peg belay in the wall above) or better, move diagonally L. up a slab until it is possible to step 6 ft. L. to a stance on Charity (peg belay high above).

4   60 ft.   From the Faith stance, traverse L. for 15 ft. and then climb up grooves until a ledge leads L. to the top, or from Charity stance, finish straight up broken quartzy rock to the terrace without much difficulty.

From the stance at the top of the Faith Cat Walk, it is possible to finish via Saint's Wall (VD) *by descending under the wall to the* R. *until a large grass ledge can be reached. From here an escape up to the* R. *is easy,* but instead the route takes the steep wall by a series of niches joined by mantel-shelves.

31 Tennis Shoe
S— 460 ft. * Odell, 1919.
This fine route takes a line near the L. hand edge of the Slabs and gains a sense of exposure from its position. In rubbers, on a warm day, it may be found a little easier than its standard suggests. Generally delicate slab climbing, except for the last pitch, which has a more serious air to it.

Start at a subsidiary slab a few ft. round the corner to the L., about 20 yds. from the Ordinary Route, although a hard start (VS) can be made up the very edge of the Slabs. Do not confuse the correct start with another slab around the corner; this is Hargreaves' Slab, a 60 ft. VD— by its L. edge.

1   90 ft.   Step up and round to the base of a smooth slab. Climb this delicately near its L. edge until it is possible to move round onto a ledge with two belays (tape is best here).

2   50 ft.   Swing out into the scoop on the R., move up past a detached block (runner) and then step out onto the slab proper. Step up to the R., then straight up delicately to reach a good ledge and low nut belay.

3   60 ft.   Step back onto the slabs and go up the edge on small but good holds to reach a spikey stance. Belay in a crack behind or step down L. and use spikes.

4   110 ft.   Get onto the L. hand rib of the gully as early as possible and follow the slabs above, keeping L. to reach a rounded ledge. Nut belay low on the R.

5   100 ft.   Another pitch up the slabs to the L. to reach a grass terrace. Belays obscure, a nut in a pocket in the wall is best.

Now walk across the ledge to belay below the final tower.

6   50 ft.   Get onto the face of the tower by a ledge and move up the edge on small polished holds. An awkward pull up on minute finger holds leads to better foot holds and, in a move, to a scoop. Up this scoop, exposed, then on to a final slab and over the perched block to finish.

32   Lazarus (Holly Tree Wall)

*S— 150 ft. * Hicks (?)*

The Holly Tree Wall is divided into two sections by
a deep gully on the R. side, above the usual finish to
Hope and Faith. This route starts in the gully but
then breaks out L. and, by some exposed climbing,
provides the easiest way up the wall.

Start on a grass ledge directly below the gully, a
few ft. of climbing above the terrace.

1   50 ft.   Climb the gully over two rock steps,
turning each one from the L., to a large recess and
chockstone belay. (The gully can be continued to the
L. by a hard mantel-shelf, Javelin Gully, s+).

2   60 ft.   Step L. round a block and then up a
little. Now traverse L. again, delicately, for 30 ft. to
reach a loose hold and then a slight corner. A rounded
spike high in the corner gives some aid and possible
protection for this, the crux, until a move R. and then
up leads to a niche. It is possible to find good belays
here, a high spike and good nuts, and so, to watch
the second on this hard section. Otherwise continue,
for the major difficulty is over.

3   40 ft.   Step up and then R. to reach easier
ground, then straight up to reach a wide terrace.
Belay well back.

Above lies the continuation wall with Groove
Above (VD+), the obvious continuation to this route.
It starts 20 ft. L. of the final belay of Lazarus and is
hard to start.

33   Original Route (Holly Tree Wall)

*S+ or VS. 140 ft. ** Richards, Holland, Miss Pilley,
1918.*

Behind and slightly L. of the perched block at the
top of Charity is another great block with a thread
belay in it. This route goes from this block up to an
obvious crack which once contained the Holly Tree,
and so direct to the top. It is a difficult route with
only fair protection.

Start at the thread belay at the block.

4   60 ft.   Step from the block up to footholds
below a scoop and attempt to get into this and so
reach a small cave under a bulge (VS). Better,
although less traditional, climb up R. onto a quartz
pinnacle, step R. and mantel-shelf up into some

pockets (thread runner in these), then repeat the move back L. and so up to the cave. From the cave continue up R.-wards by the Crescent Slab on nice holds to a rib and good stance below and to the R. of the crack. Peg belay or thread in the back of the cracks.

2 40 ft. Step down a little to the L. and so reach a rake leading out across the face. At the end of this, move up delicately for a good hold out R. and so to the rocky stance above the crack.

Or the crack can be climbed at vs standard.

3 40 ft. Continue direct up the corner layback, then easier cracks to the top (or variants further L.).

Starting from the same block as Original Route, but going up the wall well to the L. is Cinderella, a good s —.

34 Javelin Buttress (Holly Tree Wall)
*VS— 130 ft. * Graham, Jerram, 1925.*
This fine route climbs the smooth buttress to the R. of the Gully. It gives very open climbing on perfect rock.

Start at the R. hand end of the terrace, a ledge leads R. to below a groove.

1 70 ft. Go up into the groove and climb this with good holds until a slab leads out L. Climb this on pockmarks for a few ft. (Do not continue, for this is Javelin Blade, a HVS of great difficulty). Then traverse R. across to a natural thread belay and poor stance. (The excellent terrace, 10 ft. below and to the R., is the Balcony.)

2 30 ft. (But seems further). Step up R. to reach a narrow mantel-shelf. Move onto this (the crux), then continue with another difficult move to a good stance.

3 30 ft. More easily up the L. edge (or anywhere) to the terrace.

The Balcony can be reached from below direct via Balcony Cracks (vs) which starts on a subsidiary terrace to the R. of the main one. Its continuation leaves the R. side of the Balcony by cracks leading up L. in the higher part of the wall and so to the upper terrace.

This upper terrace can be left in a variety of ways. Either by a traverse L. to join the usual way off just before its final rise, or by a diagonal descent R. to reach grass above an evil looking gully, which can be avoided by further traversing to reach a hidden gully below a distant cairn. Alternatively one may climb one of the routes up the wall above (Continuation Wall) of which Groove Above is the best.

35   Rowan Tree Slabs Direct (West Wall)

HVS— 150 ft. * Hicks, Cooper, Jones, 1929.
This delightfully delicate climb goes up the West Wall looking for difficulty amongst the easy breaks. It finds it in an advanced form and so gives slab climbing at near the limit of friction on the smallest of holds.

Start as for Sub-Wall Climb, a poor v D a few ft. R. of Faith, or take the start of Faith. Either way, start on the R.-most set of slab about 70 yds. from the Ordinary Route.

1   100 ft.   Take either line up the slab to a large grass ledge (solo).

2   90 ft.   From the R. side of this ledge go up an open groove until two steps R. lead to a bulge at the bottom of a thin diagonal ramp, lightly coated with quartz and sloping up L. Get onto this with difficulty and balance up it to reach slightly better pockety holds on the wall above its end. Up these to reach a grass rake and a good belay below a crack.

· Wrong Route (v D) uses the last few ft. of this pitch, reaching it from the L. and continues up the crack above the stance.

3   60 ft.   Step out L. onto the slabs and then up these on small holds. After 25 ft. one could traverse back R. to the crack (the old way) but it seems more fitting to continue L. on pockets with difficulty and lack of protection, until a long reach makes the final few ft. climbable.

From the stance above, on a large grass ledge, it is possible to step round L. and then either slant up easily L. (Wrong Route) to reach Saint's Wall, or climb the steep corner above (Sinner's Corner, v s).

36   Heather Wall (East Wall)

VS. 170 ft. * Hicks, Hargreaves, Stewardson, 1929.
The East Wall is in three main sections; the lowest one being the wall which gives exposure to all the lower pitches of Tennis Shoe. Then, almost at right-angles to this is a bulging, water streaked wall which drops from the final tower of Tennis Shoe, and is dominated by the perched block, and finally, a

blank area of wall running from a long diagonal
groove up to the way off.

The lowest section, which contains this route, is
bounded on the R. by the first pitch of Tennis Shoe,
and on the L. by a corner (Rake End Chimney, s −)
which is reached from below by a diagonal rake The
route is one of the best on the wall, on clean rock
and using delightful pocket holds. The crux is well
situated near the top.

Start below the lower end of the rake where a
grassy ledge bisects the easy slabs of the descent
routes, about 200 ft. up from the start of Tennis Shoe.
Also the start of Heather Weakness (v D +) and Rake
End Chimney (s −).

1   100 ft.   Go R. on a little gangway (after 10 ft.
Rake End Chimney goes up), and continue until a
line of holds leads up the wall with occasional moves
L., and then higher, back R., to reach a smooth cone
of slab which runs up the steep wall above. Go up to
the apex of this cone and then step L. to reach a poor
stance, and spike belay or peg.

Heather Weakness climbs some of this pitch but
avoids difficulties to the R., and on reaching the slab,
steps round the corner to a good stance on the R.

2   70 ft.   It is possible to continue straight up, but
much better to traverse L. to reach a grassy groove.
Cross this and up the rib beyond, tending L. Either
go up over the bulge direct, or traverse L. again
(usually wet) to a good foothold and thread runners,
and then pull up R. over the bulge (slightly easier
and safer). Now step up L. into a groove and follow
this R. to a good stance with devious belays. *Tennis
Shoe lies just over the ridge and can be crossed to reach the
Ordinary Route and this descended.*

37   Ash Tree Slab (East Wall)

*S. 170 ft. * Hicks, Smalley, 1929.*
This fine route takes the second facet of the East
Wall, directly below the perched block of Tennis
Shoe. Well protected and on excellent holds it is,
however, sometimes very wet.

Start at the top of the second section of broken
slab about 100 ft. above Heather Wall start. The
climb takes the centre of the wall above, and so a
stance and belay should be taken below it.

1.   100 ft.   Go straight up the wall on excellent
holds to below the bulge at 50 ft.; go round this on

the R. (awkward) and then move up slabbier rock to a ledge with good belays at its L. end.

2 40 ft. Step L. for 4 ft. and then go up on good holds, dodging between any remaining grass ledges, to reach a stance below and to the L. of the final tower.

3 30 ft. Many finishes are possible to the L. and direct, but the best traverses R. onto the tower and then makes a hard move up and round to join Tennis Shoe for its last few ft.

38 East Wall Girdle

*S+ 510 ft. ** Edwards, Palmer, 1931.*

This enjoyable route collects all the delights of the East Wall into one climb. It is possible in most conditions, for most of the holds are positive and, if climbed in boots and carrying sacks, as part of a full mountain day, and followed by Lazarus, Groove Above and Grey Slab on Glyder Fawr, it can give a good pair of climbers an Alpine training session of great value. It attempts to follow a line midway up the wall for its complete length.

Start at the foot of Tennis Shoe, 40 ft. L. of the Ordinary Route.

1 90 ft. As for Tennis Shoe. The L. edge of the slab. Tape belays.

2 30 ft. Continue direct up the grassy quartz slab without difficulty. Spike belay near a tree.

3 110 ft. Take the crack above the belay, then delicately up the grooves above with odd runners in the corner. A long stride L. brings the cone of the slab of Heather Wall into reach and this is followed to its top. Next step L. to a belay as for Heather Wall. Peg or spike.

4 40 ft. Traverse L., then diagonally L. and across a wet patch as for Heather Wall. However, avoid its crux by stepping down to reach a grass ledge. Traverse L. for 15 ft. from this to reach a stance at the top of the rake of Rake End Chimney.

5 70 ft. Step up a few ft. and then step across, round two slight corners to reach the slab part of Ash Tree Slab. Climb these slabs L. then back R. to reach a pair of belays at the L. end of a ledge.

6 90 ft. Traverse low round the corner and keep low to reach an area of grass ledges. Follow rock then grass to a stance below a final rock wall on the L.

7 80 ft. From near the belay, climb a crack to reach

a large runner. Move L. from this and then go up on spaced holds to a small stance (40 ft.). Step L. from this stance into an exposed groove and climb this delicately to its top. Good belay 10 ft. further.

This final pitch is the top section of Grooved Wall (S), which reaches the stance below, up grooves under the grass ledges.

10 ft. before the end of this last pitch, it is possible to step L. to a flake and so, via an abseil, continue the traverse. This section, the traverse of Suicide Wall is very hard (ES−) and out of context in this route.

39   Suicide Wall Route 1

ES−   100 ft. ** *Preston, Morsley, Haines, 1945.*
This route takes the steep, smooth section of wall below the highest part of the way off. This wall is bounded on the R. by a steep diagonal groove (Suicide Groove, HVS) and on the L. by a small gully. This route takes a line to the L. of the centre on which the only real feature is a grass ledge. It is very sustained on small pocket holds and protection is only fair. No direct aid is needed, but a protective piton is usual, and indeed sensible.

Start below and to the L. of the grass ledge. Many scratches!

1   100 ft.   Step up a little R. and then make a very hard move up to a little spike in a pocket (the hardest move on the route), and use this, and another little pocket to reach slightly easier climbing (**Plate 12**), and so the grass ledge. On the first ascent, all three climbers gathered here and belayed to a tent peg in the grass! However, it is better to use a sling to place, or clip into a peg, high on the L., for protection, and then to descend to the ledge for a smoke. When ready, step R. to a rib and scoop and move up this for 8 ft., then back L. above the ledge to better holds. Now move diagonally R. on improving holds to step into a final break, and up this to grass and the top.

Suicide Wall Route 2 (ES−) takes a fault between this and the groove using obvious spikes and a peg to reach its crux, a smooth scoop. It finishes up a slab just L. of the top of the Groove.

Cwm Idwal. Upper Cliff of Glyder Fawr

*N. Facing. 2,250 ft. above sea level. 300 ft. high +
scrambling. G.R. 644586.*

Plate 12. First section of Suicide Wall-Route 1

This cliff, as its name suggests, lies high on the N. face of Glyder Fawr, above and to the R. of Idwal Slabs. Its base lies about 400 ft. higher than the top of Continuation Wall, and can be reached from there by an enjoyable scramble up problems plus an 80 ft. pitch up a pocketed slab (Lava Slab VD), and then by a traverse over quartz ledges. If a direct approach is required, either go well past the Idwal Slabs and then labour up the screes, or take Idwal Buttress (D—), an easy climb up the nose of rock to the R. of the slabs. It lies just R. of the nasty gully which the R. hand descent avoids, and just before the screes. Via the screes it takes an hr. from Ogwen.

Parking and mountain rescue facilities as for Bochlwyd Buttress.

The crag itself is rather broken, with its main features being two grassy gullies with a slabby nose between them. These are East Gully (VD), Central Gully (S), and East Arête (D), the only pleasant route of the three, and even it deteriorates higher. However, a few hundred ft. to the L. of East Gully lies an area of good, steep, grey rock and it is here that the best routes lie, the Grey Group. Finally, to the R. of the R. hand gully lies an arête, whose edge is quite well defined, Central Arête.

The Grey Group give superb climbing on fine rough rock. The lines of the routes are individual and pitches once started give little option of escape. A place for mountaineering skills as well as rock gymnastic ability. In contrast, the Central Arête is a more Alpine climb.

40 Grey Slab
*S+ 270 ft. *** Edwards, Reade, 1932.*
The Grey Group presents two main facets. A slab starting in a wet corner, and a wall, split by cracks in its upper part, which lies to the R. of the corner, with a fine arête almost overhanging the slab. To the L. of the slab, a blunt rib goes up the lower part of the cliff (Grey Rib, S—). Grey Slab starts up the wet corner, then moves out onto the slab proper. It is a great route, delicate and sustained throughout its second pitch, with only a little protection.

Start at the foot of the corner.
1   120 ft.   Climb the corner for 90 ft., easily at first, but soon becoming quite difficult, and a little grassy. Where the grass is profuse, move out L. onto some

pock marks and use these to reach a ledge. From the
L. end of the ledge, an awkward move up a small
corner leads to a poor stance with excellent belays
below an overhang.

2   150 ft.   Pull over the bulge and go up a few
feet to a runner. Next traverse L. on small holds until
holds, widely spaced, lead up a faint rib. At the end
of this is a good foothold, from which delicate moves
take one up onto a slab below another overlap, and
this little ramp of slab is followed up to the L. Near its
end, traverse R. with difficulty (possibly the crux
although it is all hard) to reach a line of pockets leading
up (often wet). Follow these to a stance and poor
belay. Possibly continue 40 ft. more to a better stance.

*From the top, either scramble on up to the summit (600 ft.)
or traverse L. to reach the upper level of the Nameless Cwm.*

41   Grey Arête

HVS 270 ft. ** *James, Benson, 1959.*
This route follows the edge of the wall to the R. of
Grey Slab. It has good position, continuously interesting and difficult climbing and seems to be one of the
best routes in the area.

Start on the same ledge as Grey Slab, below a
scoop which blunts the arête initially.

1   120 ft.   Step into the scoop and follow this by
semi-layback for 15 ft. until a slab can be reached by
a step R. Now climb this near the edge, becoming
easier, to reach a good stance. Belay a little to the R.
as for the start of Grey Wall, a VS which climbs the
R. half of this face via twin cracks.

2   40 ft.   Step L. from the belay, then go up the
middle of the pock marked wall, until a step L. leads
to a small rock stance near the edge. Chockstone or
nut belay.

3   80 ft.   Up the steep crack above by layback
until a hard move leads to a small grass ledge.
Continue to layback up L. until the flake-crack leans
back R. Step awkwardly into it and follow it to a
grass ledge above with a belay well to the R.

4   30 ft.   The easier wall above the crack provides
a pleasant finish.

42   Central Arête Direct

VD 320 ft. **w** *Mrs Daniell, Barlow 1909.*
This route lies up the ridge to the R. of Central
Gully. It gives quite difficult climbing for the first

130 ft. and then, a ridge of pinnacles and flakes at a more gentle standard, takes one high onto the mountain.

Start just on the arête.

1   120 ft.   Straight up the arête on small holds, getting harder at the top. Quite steep and exposed to a stance on the R.

2   50 ft.   Traverse up to the L. until the easier normal route is joined.

3   150 ft.   The rest of the route lies up the arête, over spikes and pinnacles, until it merges into the hillside.

From the first stance one can look R. at a slab crossed by a diagonal line of pock marks. This is Great West Slab, a VS of some difficulty but little point.

Cwm Idwal. Clogwyn Y Geifr
NE. Facing. 2,000 ft. above sea level. 250 ft. high.
G.R. 639589.

These, the cliffs around the Devil's Kitchen, lie at the head of the Cwm, and are easily reached by the footpath from Ogwen to Nant Peris, which cuts through the cliffs. Comfortably reached in 40 mins.

Parking and mountain rescue facilities as for Bochlwyd Buttress.

The crag is divided naturally into four parts by the two footpaths which go up L. or R. from the foot of the Kitchen, and by the Kitchen itself. These divisions give a S. cliff, mostly loose and wet; a central cliff in two halves, to the L. grassy and uninviting, to the R., steeper and better and cut by two gullies; finally, a N. cliff low down on the R., steep and smooth with grass to its R. The whole cliff needs much traffic before it becomes a good climbing ground, but climbers must remember that the cliff is of great interest to the naturalist, and so vegetation should be undisturbed. Character and an air of tradition are not lacking on these routes, and a simple grab and rubber-up technique will not suffice here. In winter, some of the gullies and cracks yield ice routes of a high standard, and these cliffs then become a place to polish ice technique rather than to learn it!

43   The Devil's Kitchen. Twll Du
VD+ 100 ft. of climbing. * **w** *Reade, McCulloch, 1898.*

This route, one of the great classics, gains its merit, not from difficulty or beauty of technique, but by its unique situation. Done in nails, on a day of storm, with the great waterfall in full spate, it gives greater satisfaction than many VS routes climbed in good weather. It wanders into the depths of the Kitchen (a trip many could enjoy) and then escapes up the L. wall by quite steep climbing.

Start at the mouth of the chasm.

1 Scramble up the bed of the stream to reach the first problem, a large boulder blocking the gully.

2 20 ft. The Waterfall Pitch. Up on the R. (the easiest), on the L. (hard work), or through a tunnel (usually very wet).

3 Now continue easily up the bed past pools and a great leaning pinnacle on the R. wall, until a capstone blocks the gully causing the waterfall.

4 80 ft. 'The Great Pitch'. 20 ft. before the waterfall, cracks slant up the L. wall to the level of the capstone. Reach these cracks and use them, on large holds, to reach an awkward traversing line which takes one onto the capstone.

5 Easy walking remains.

44 Advocate's Wall

*VS+ 200 ft. * Preston, Morsley, McKellar, 1945.*
This very good route lies within the Kitchen on its R. wall. The rock is usually good although protection is difficult to find, whilst the overall ambience leaves little to be desired!

Start just below the Waterfall Pitch, beneath the big overhangs on the R. wall.

1 60 ft. Climb up the corner and then across the black slab to reach an overhanging ledge. Thread belay.

2 70 ft. Go up for about 10 ft. and then traverse with difficulty around the corner L. (the crux) onto a face and up this.

3 70 ft. Climb a chimney, then exposed rocks on the L. to the top.

On the opposite side of the Kitchen at the same level lies another good route of similar character, Pilgrim's Progress (S+).

45 Devil's Staircase

*S— 285 ft. ** w Jones, Abraham, 1899.*
To the R. of the Kitchen lies a grassy buttress, Devil's

Buttress (vD), defined on its R. by the steep line of a chimney which forks near the top. This chimney gives one of the best routes on the cliff and indeed, one of the best gullies in this guide.

Start at the foot of the gully.

1   **85 ft.**   Climb up easily for a few ft., then step into a narrow, shallow chimney which is hard for 20 ft. Continue past good runners to a large ledge, go on higher to a better one.

2   **110 ft.**   Climb up the L. side for 30 ft. until after passing two large blocks, a cave is reached. Climb up more easily for 40 ft. (runner) and then move out L. round the overhang, and continue up the bed to a stance.

3   **90 ft.**   A hard finish goes up the L. crack above, but it is better to reach the R. one by the wall below it, and so dive into a deep crack (the Drainpipe), and climb up inside this past a chockstone, to reappear in the upper part at a stance.

Scrambling now remains.

46   Hanging Garden Gully

VD 290 ft. **w** *Jones, Abraham Bros. 1899.*

This route is included because of its great botanical interest rather than the beauty of its climbing. It is a gully in which vegetation has grown in remarkable profusion and variety. It lies 200 ft. R. of Devil's Staircase, and is the most conspicuous gully on that part of the cliff.

Start at the foot of the gully, where the path begins to steepen.

1   **150 ft.**   Easy climbing up the gully bed followed by a grass walk.

2   **20 ft.**   To the L. is a short crack which is usually wet. Climb this on good holds.

3   **120 ft.**   The Great Pitch. This climbs the R. hand branch of the gully, first by climbing the R. wall, then easy climbing to a cave at 60 ft., and finally, the best part of the route, a steep 'juggy' crack to the top.

50   Devil's Nordwand

HVS— 380 ft. * *James, Anthoine, 1959.*

This route, as its name suggests, lies on the North Cliff, on an area of smoother, steeper rock than the rest of the Kitchen cliffs. This impressive cliff had, for many years, only two routes, both vs—, Devil's

Dive and North Slabs, creeping up the grassy R. hand edge, but recently, four routes have been discovered, all around HVS, of which the one described was the first, and has had the most ascents. It is an excellent line up the centre of the crag on good rock.

Start. In the centre of the crag about 60 ft. up and just L. of an obvious groove (The Druid's Doghouse, HVS) is a 10 ft. square niche. Start directly below this.

1 60 ft. Climb the face of the indefinite pedestal until forced into the grassy crack on the left. Climb this easily to the top.

2 100 ft. Ascend a thin crack for 10 ft., and then traverse L. to the niche. Leave it by the top L. hand corner, and step L., then diagonally R. to a small grass ledge. From its R. extremity step up a crack, and then go diagonally R. up a thin slab to a stance and peg belay.

3 100 ft. Descend the previous pitch for a few moves and then make a semi hand traverse L. to a heather ledge. Climb direct to an open chimney, go up this to another sloping slab and peg belay.

4 120 ft. Easily up the wall to the L. for 40 ft., then up steeply on big holds until it is possible to step R. onto a grass ledge. Up R., then back L. to top.

Two other good routes, God's Little Acre and Junior Slab lie up the walls to the L. of this route. They are both HVS −. On the band of crag above the Devil's Nordward and to its L. can be seen a clean steep arête which gives fine climbing at VS+ standard, Devil's Delight.

The Carneddau. Braich Ty Ddu

W. Facing. 1,200 ft. above sea level. From 100 − 250 ft. high. G.R. 649609

This area of broken buttresses lies on Pen Yr Oleu Wen, above the main A 5 road, between Ogwen and Tyn Y Maes. Although there seems to be a great deal of rock, little of it is of interest. However, the routes selected offer a change from the well worn Milestone Buttress and Cwm Idwal routes, and are in the sun, even in winter. They are reached best from Ogwen Falls by ascending a few ft. above the Alfred Embleton stile and then following a faint traversing path. Their order of description applies when they are approached from this direction. Time from

Ogwen to the farthest route is under 30 mins.

Mountain rescue and parking facilities as for Bochlwyd Buttress, plus extra parking on laybys below the crag.

The routes described lie on a series of buttresses which are in fact the ends of faint spurs dropping from high on the mountain. They were distinguished originally in alphabetical order, but some appear to have vanished, so they will be described as one reaches them along the path.

48   Widdershins

S+ 250 ft. Moulam, McNaught-Davis, 1950.
After leaving the road the first climbable rock is on the R. and very near. This is Pont Pen Y Benglog Buttress (also known as Exhibiton Buttress), and gives a D− up the front and harder problems round on the R. However, if one traverses L, after 80 yds. one passes a small, grooved buttress with a vs+ up the groove to a large overhang. 70 yds. further, a trace of a dry stone wall comes against the first real crag (G. Buttress) with an obviously hard route (Apprentice's Route, HVS) up the front and then out R. round the overhang. However, a few yds. L. the rock is less steep and 200 ft. up this side is a rowan tree amongst piled blocks, and 30 ft. above this tree a fine holly tree can be seen on a ledge.

Start above the first tree on the terrace formed by the blocks.

1   30 ft.   Easily up to the holly tree.

2   45 ft.   Climb the steep crack with difficulty (crux), then easy slabs to a ledge with a belay on the L.

3   50 ft.   Step L. and climb a corner crack for a few ft., then make a step L. into another crack. Up this to a stance above on a detached flake.

4   75 ft.   Climb a chimney on the L. moving out L. at the top, to a flat grassy ledge. Then a short corner on the L. leads to a final short wall and a bollard belay.

5   50 ft.   25 ft. across, slightly R., is a clean crack in a slab. Climb it to near the top and then make a delicate finger traverse L. and so to large blocks and a large stance.
Way off is to the L. via a heather scramble.

49   Pinnacle Ridge

VD. 320 ft. Ingold, Miss Fearon, Ball. 1950

From the foot of G. Buttress, continue following the path across the steep hillside. Soon a spur intrudes and a grassy gully leads out onto exposed grass slopes; descend these and continue round the corner on very rich grass to the lowest point of all the crags. Climb up a few ft. to below an obvious clean cut ridge leading in its upper part to a castellated ridge. This is the route.

Start at the foot. (This is F. Buttress).

1   100 ft.   Very delicate steps up the very edge of the ridge for a few ft. lead to better holds. After 60 ft. a large block is reached and from this an awkward high step leads into a groove on the R., and so to easier ground with a stance and large spike belays.

2   70 ft.   A square cut groove on the R. leads to heather scrambling. Continue to a spike belay.

3   75 ft.   Traverse across R. until good holds lead up to a ridge; follow this easily to a stance on its R. side.

4   75 ft.   Climb up steeply from the stance on to the crest and go over or round pinnacles until a final down and up lead to the top. A photogenic pitch.

50   Decameron Rib

VS — 180 ft. * Lane, Boydell, 1955.

From the foot of Pinnacle Ridge continue the traverse until, a few hundred ft. up the hillside, a fine buttress can be seen, with a great square-cut roof at half height. This is E. (?) Buttress and the route climbs through the overhang. It is the best climb on the cliff.

Start. Various possibilities are obvious (**Plate 13**). However, the one described is of the right standard, and lies up the short chimney 15 ft. R. of the foot of the groove which leads to the overhang.

1   90 ft.   Climb the chimney for 15 ft. then traverse into the groove and continue up this to the roof. Step out L. to a stance and belay in the chimney splitting the roof.

2   90 ft.   Climb the chimney and then go up for a few ft. on the R. Soon a diagonal groove leads L. to

below a knife edged hanging flake. Either climb this (possibly dangerous) or step L. to pass it, and via a slab to a good stance.

3 30 ft. A good step L. leads up to a final pinnacle which can be climbed. Then step across to easy ground.

Rather than descend it is better to scramble up L. for 200 ft. until a traverse leads into an easy gully. This is the gully in which the next climb starts.

51 B Buttress. Route 2
S. 120 ft. Palmer, Furlonge, 1927.
From the foot of Decameron Rib, an easy wide gully leads up L. with rock walls appearing on each side. B Buttress lies on the L., but on the R. there are also some interesting climbs; a poised block (tea chest size) provides the point of Temptation (s−) whilst Patience (VD) takes the excellent rib on its L. However, Route 2 lies higher that these on the L., starting on the R. of the Buttress at a cairn below a corner full of jammed blocks. Do not confuse the start of Route 1 (VD) which is also cairned and lies at the lowest point of this buttress by a detached flake. Our start is 40 ft. to the R. of this.

1 40 ft. Up the jammed blocks.

2 25 ft. Continue by an open chimney and leave this with difficulty on the R. with aid from a horizontal spike. Stance and belay above.

3 60 ft. Climb the steep quartz wall above on excellent holds.

52 Cuckoo Groove
HVS. 150 ft. * Lees, Wilkinson, 1960.
This is a good route taking the groove 30 ft. R. of Route 2. It gives continually hard climbing on excellent rock.
    Start at a 10 ft. pinnacle.

1 50 ft. Enter the groove with difficulty (or aid) and climb it to a poor stance on the L. Fair belays. A peg is better.

2 50 ft. Step back down and move out on to the R. edge. Successive hard moves lead up to a stance.

3 50 ft. Climb up into the overhanging corner and escape R. by a layback to easier ground.

Plate 13.
Decameron Rib by an easier start. The climb next goes under the big roof

Another hard route, Peacock Wall (HVS), takes the overhanging wall to the R. of this route, and then the steep crack to the R. of the second stance.

The Carneddau. Llech Ddu

N. Facing. 1,900 ft. above sea level. 600 ft. maximum height. G.R. 663638

This superb crag lies at the end of a spur of Carnedd Dafydd, on the R. of Cwm Llafar a little before the crags of Black Ladders are reached. It can be reached from Ogwen by descending the A5 road to the farm of Ty Gwyn (GR 642625), and then by following a well marked track up the hillside to reach the long northern shoulder of Pen Yr Oleu Wen. The area of level, marshy ground is now crossed in an easterly direction to a col, and a descent made into the cwm where the alternative path, which starts from Gerlan Water Works (GR 638658), can be joined. This path peters out at a marshy stream bifurcation, and the crag can be reached in about ten mins. up the hillside. Total time from Ogwen, about 1 hr., or from Gerlan, about 50 mins.

Parking is possible in laybys just above Ty Gwyn, but is difficult in the Gerlan approach, although the odd car may be left in the farm yard of Gwaun Y Gwiail with the farmer's consent. Otherwise, park in the village.

Mountain rescue facilities are as for Bochlwyd Buttress. It is quickest to summon help by sending a message to the Water Works house in Gerlan asking them to telephone Ogwen Cottage Mountain Rescue Team or, better, letting the message bearer speak himself.

The cliff itself is triangular, very steep, but split by a grassy traverse line which rises high in the centre of the crag, and which divides it into three separate sections. In the centre lies a great triangular buttress topped by twin pinnacles. This buttress stops 200 ft. below the top of the cliff, and is broken by a grassy ledge coming in quite low from the R. Above the buttress, and to its L., above another great area of grass, is a very steep wall on which there is the great square roof of the Great Corner, whilst to the R. of the central buttress is another area of steep chimneys and grooves which looks deceptively easy.

The routes selected on this crag are all extremely

Plate 14. The Groove on Llech D'du, pitch 3

hard, for it is only on the steep rock that vegetation has not lasted. Some of these routes are the best in the area, and indeed in this guide. Two lie on the central area and present excellent problems of groove climbing, whilst the one on the L. section, the Great Corner, is one of the best corner climbs in Britain. These routes seem to take a fair amount of time, and some very good parties have been known to bivouac due to miscalculations of this type. However, the combining of Central Route with the Great Corner, or the Groove with Commuter's Crack or one of its neighbours, gives a better day's climbing than many Dolomite free climbs.

53 Central Route

*VS. 410 ft. ** Dwyer, Morsley, 1946.*
This is the easiest of the four routes to be described, yet still provides climbing of an excellent nature with the first two pitches being steep and continually interesting. The upper section, although easier, visits some delightful situations. It climbs the L. hand groove on the face of the central pillar, the only weakness to the L. of the obvious central groove.

Start above two large boulders on the path below a small V-chimney.

1 **100 ft.** Get up into the V-chimney and back up it until a rib leads up R. Follow this until a steep bulge appears above. A hard step L. onto an overhang leads in a few ft. to a stance below the groove.

2 **100 ft.** Climb the corner crack to a grass (?) ledge below overhangs. Now swing out on to the R. wall and move round onto a slab. Up this to a belay on the top.

3 **30 ft.** Up the crack behind the flake until a grassy semi hand traverse leads L. to reach a central grass break.

The start of the Great Corner lies 120 ft. to the L. across steep grass.

4 **90 ft.** Up the easy chimney to the L. hand top of the central pillar (The Pinnacle).

5 **90 ft.** Various possibilities exist around the overhang above. The one to its L. is the easiest. Alternatively, traverse R. to the other top (The Pillar) and ascend grass and some good rock, tending R. for nearly 300 ft. (Central Slab Route, VD+).

If time is short, descend the chimney on the R. of the Pillar and then continue traversing and descending steep grass to reach the foot of the crag (this is the approach to Route 56 in reverse).

54   The Groove

ES— 375 ft. *** Anthoine and Campbell, 1961.
This magnificent route takes the challenge of the great groove which is the most obvious feature of the central part of the cliff. The first ascent involved extensive gardening which explains the fact that five days were taken, and a fair amount of aid used. Subsequent ascents needed less aid and in fact, the two protective pitons in place, plus one sling used for direct aid on the loose and damp section seem to be a reasonable way to climb it now.

Start below a crack, slightly R. of the line of the groove about 80 ft. from Central Route.

1   75 ft.   Up the corner past an old piton at 40 ft., to move L. onto grass and via this up to a tree.

2   60 ft.   Behind the tree is a groove blocked by a poised flake. Climb up past this carefully to reach a niche below a loose, often greasy bulge. Use a sling to climb this onto the R. wall, which is followed to an uncomfortable stance. It is better to continue for a few feet and thread one rope through a ring attached to a piton high above. This helps to protect the next pitch both for leader and second, and also makes the stance a little safer.

3   90 ft.   Traverse L. delicately on small holds (**Plate 14**) to reach the groove itself and climb this for 30 ft. to reach a stance. Peg belay.

4   100 ft.   Climb the groove past three difficult sections until it eases and a grass stance is reached. A grand pitch which is especially exciting for the badly placed second.

5   50 ft.   Move out onto the R. wall and up this on excellent holds to reach grass and so the top of the Pillar.

Escape as for Central Route.

55   The Great Corner

ES— 230 ft. ** Clements and Potts, 1965.
This route, which climbs the obvious corner in the L. part of the upper crag, and then turns the great overhang by some sensational climbing, is a superb route, well placed, high on this very steep crag. Start at the foot of the corner. It can be reached by ascending Central Route (53, the best) or by following one

of the grassy traverses and grooves from below (this seems dangerous).

1   130 ft.   Climb the corner easily at first, then getting harder until a piton gives aid for a few ft., then a crack leads up to a bridging stance under the roof, level with a large detached flake.

2   100 ft.   Traverse L., past the flake, to reach the the arête. Step round this (out of sight and often out of hearing of the second) and descend a few ft. to reach the foot of a crack. (There is another one to the L., ignore it!) Climb the crack which is very hard and usually needs aid from a sling, or even two, until a jamming crack through the main roof can be reached. Follow this and a groove above to a grassy slab and the top. An exciting and difficult pitch which could give rope work problems.

The wall to the L. of this route provides another hard route, Endor (E S −) which climbs the L. hand of two grooves.

56   Commuter's Crack

*HVS. 310 ft. * Hatton, Jones and Moulam, 1966.*
The R. hand section of the cliff above the easy traversing line which leads to the top of the Pillar, is steep and split by various grooves and chimneys. The most noticeable is on the R. and is Y Chimney which, if taken direct, gives a good VS climb, whilst higher on the traverse, about 50 ft. to the L., is an open groove of lighter rock, the line of Elliw (HVS). Just L. of this an easier line of cracks and grooves gives Humour, a varied VS. However, the best of the routes on this section of cliff is Commuter's Crack which climbs the crack on the L. wall of the arête to the R. of Elliw.

Start on the slab below Elliw (also the start of Humour).

1   120 ft.   Go up R. to enter the crack awkwardly. A sling may be needed higher, but then steep but easier climbing leads to a poor stance with thread belays.

2   60 ft.   Continue in a steep groove for 30 ft., then on steep grass.

3   40 ft.   More grass on the R. to a belay below a steep slab.

4   90 ft.   Take the slab direct to finish on good holds.

The Carneddau. Craig Yr Ysfa

NE. Facing. 2,000 ft. above sea-level. 800 ft. high.
G.R. 694637.

The large crag lies at the head of Cwm Eigiau, high
on the flanks of Carnedd Llywelyn. It can be approached direct up the cwm from Dolgarrog, it
being possible to drive to the dam on Llyn Eigiau,
but more usually, it is approached from the A5 road,
between Helyg and Gwern Y Gof Isaf, by a very
straight path which leads first to Ffynon Llugwy and
then climbs the steep head wall to the col between
Pen Yr Helgi Du and Carnedd Llywelyn. From this
col the top of the crag can be seen on the R. shoulder
of Llywelyn, Pinnacle Wall climb being quite obvious.
For the Amphitheatre Wall routes it is probably better
to ascend to the top of the cliff via the ridge and deposit
rucksacks etc. there, whilst for the longer, easier routes
a path leads down to the foot of the crag from the col.
By any of these routes it is difficult to reach the start of
a climb in under one hr. from either Ogwen or Dolgarrog.

Parking is rather limited on the Ogwen side, but
ample at the dam of Llyn Eigiau.

Mountain rescue arrangements are rather complex
for this cliff. Accidents to parties low on the cliff are
best reported to the Ogwen Rescue Post via a telephone (only to be used in emergencies) which can
be found at the dam of Llyn Eigiau. Those near the
top of the cliff can often be relayed by passing
walkers or spectators direct to Ogwen. For rescue
parties it is much better to approach from the Ogwen
side and to evacuate via Llyn Eigiau (or helicopter
if available).

The crag is made up of two great buttresses, separated by the Amphitheatre, from which a line of light
coloured scree runs down to near the valley floor.
The R. hand buttress is vegetated and cleft by a long,
diagonal N. facing gully (Great Gully), whilst the
L. hand buttress is cut by two gullies. The shallow R.
one forms, with the Amphitheatre, the limits of
Amphitheatre Buttress, whilst the steeper, L. one
leads up to a widening, the Cirque, which gives a
remote area of good, hard climbs which seem rarely
to be visited.

The routes described here are the most popular on
the cliff, and include classic routes of great variety,

both in character, technique and standard. Great
Gully is one of the great Welsh gullies and its ascent
in true winter conditions provides a superb climb.
Similarly, Amphitheatre Buttress gives a climb similar
to a Tryfan East Face ridge, yet more serious and
longer. Finally, the routes on the Amphitheatre Wall
give steep climbing on perfect rock in a magnificent
situation.

57 Amphitheatre Buttress

D+ 970 ft. *** w *Abraham Bros., others, 1905.*
This is a detached buttress which forms the L. side of
the Amphitheatre. It is a long mountaineering route
and one of the best of its standard in Wales.

Start at the foot of the buttress, a little above the
lowest part of the path.

1   100 ft.   Up the face of the buttress to a good
stance.

2   120 ft.   Step up onto a large block and from this,
continue via slabs and a smooth, rather difficult
groove.

3   100 ft.   Continue up cracks etc. to reach easier
rocks.

4   80 ft.   A few ft. to the R. of the edge via a slab,
then scramble up to a great heathery shelf. Belay low
down on the L. for the next pitch.

5   30 ft.   The Crux. Move up on the R. of the
arête to a good runner, step round R., exposed, and
so reach a slab. Up this to another bilberry shelf.

6   30 ft.   Climb up steeply with a semi mantel shelf
onto easy ground (another hard pitch).

7   200 ft.   Easy heathery scrambling.

8   110 ft.   The ridge now goes horizontal with a
series of pinnacles. Traverse these (**Plate 15**) and via
a gap and a sharp edge, reach the main bulk of the
mountain.

9   80 ft.   Scramble up to the foot of the final rocks.

10   120 ft.   Climb the rocks ahead, first on the R.,
then round to the L., to arrive at the top.

Plate 15. On the Pinnacles of Amphitheatre Buttress

58 Great Gully

*VD+ (in perfect conditions only). 800 ft. * w Thompson, Simey, Clay, 1900.*

This is an excellent gully climb with numerous awkward pitches, nearly all of which are avoidable. The outlook from it is good. In winter conditions it gives one of the best expeditions of its type in Wales, and can be very hard indeed.

Start at the foot of the gully, which is reached by walking round the foot of the buttress on the R. of the Amphitheatre, and past an indistinct gully to this more obvious one.

Scramble up for 150 ft.

1   10 ft.   Turn the chockstone on the L. (Many of these lower pitches are buried in winter). Scramble up for 80 ft.

2   15 ft.   Round the chockstone on the L., or up under it!   Scramble up for 80 ft.

3   50 ft.   In deep snow climb the Door Jamb. Otherwise avoid it by a steep groove on the R. and an easy traverse back to the gully.

4   15 ft.   Bridge up direct or scramble on the R.

5   30 ft.   Steep and wet up the gully bed or better, the deep chimney on the R.

6   45 ft.   The Chimney is climbed by bridging or back and foot. It is quite wide! Step out R. at the top. (All this can be missed way out on the R. wall by traverse and grass).

7   30 ft.   The R. hand groove, then scramble 80 ft. on scree.

8   20 ft.   The chimney to the R. of the rib, or the mossy chockstones on the L. Scramble for 60 ft.

9   20 ft.   The R. wall is delicate, the R. hand chimney difficult, and the L. hand chimney un-inspiring.

10   30 ft.   The Great Cave Pitch. Walk to the back of the cave. First get up onto the R. wall, and so get astride the small, inner chockstone. Move across this to the L. wall and traverse out across this to reach the outer chockstone. Scrambling to the top.

Pitches 9 and 10 can be avoided by chimneys which leave the gully just above pitch 8. The L. one is strenuous, the R. one leads to easy ground in a few ft.

59 Mur Y Niwl

*VS. 255 ft. *** w Moulam, Churchill, 1952.*

A magnificent route which takes the easiest line up

Plate 16. Hand traversing on pitch 3 of Mur Y Niwel

the lower half of the Amphitheatre Wall. The Wall
is fairly simple in structure and is best viewed initially
from just below the approach path on the top of the
buttress before (to the s.) of Amphitheatre Buttress,
or of course, from this route itself. The wall is divided
into an upper and lower section by a wide shelf, the
Bilberry Ledge, and so climbs on the lower section
may be finished by continuing up the easier part
above. The main features of the lower section are a
short diagonal crack on the L. (The Crack, HVS),
and a steep, open, R-ward sloping corner farther R.
which Mur Y Niwl visits at its base for its second
stance. Further R., the wall bulges even more, giving
the improbable line of Agrippa (HVS +). On the
upper section, the quartz traverse and the pinnacle
of Pinnacle Wall are obvious on the R., whilst
Grimmett finds its way up the overhangs a little to
the L. *The upper routes can be reached either by the gully to
the L. (loose) and then a short ascent to the Bilberry Terrace,
or better, by descending a grass gully well to the R. and then
traversing in at that end of the terrace. Similarly, the lower
routes are reached by descending the lower part of the gully.*
Mur Y Niwl climbs the lower wall in a diagonal line
from below and to the L. of an obvious grass ledge
below the open groove. Pitons are needed only for
belays.

Start in the gully bed in a small damp chimney.

1   40 ft.   Pull up on finger holds to reach a low
traverse line which leads to a grass ledge. Belay high
on the wall (or peg?).

2   40 ft.   Move up to the belay and then step R. to
use a sloping foothold to get into a small niche. Good
holds lead up to the foot of the open groove. Peg belay.

3   65 ft.   Step down a little and then either hand
or foot traverse out R. (**Plate 16**). Either method
leaves an awkward move onto a small foothold, and
then a delicate step R. to reach a diagonal crack line
with ledges. Follow these, not easy, to reach a perch
belay under a roof. Small belay or peg. (The second
can be protected by putting one rope over a
gargoyle).

4   25 ft.   Step down slightly to the R., and using a
diagonal line of sharp handholds, get onto a ledge
where the overhang finishes. Move up and step up
to the R. to a good belay. The major difficulties are
now over and one can start to enjoy the situation.

*Plate 17. First Ascent of the Girdle of the lower Amphitheatre Wall,
pitch 2*

5 35 ft. Step up L., then a high step further L. leads to a wide ledge.

6 40 ft. The crack above is awkward onto easy slabs. These lead L. to below a final little wall.

7 10 ft. The little wall. Then walk 60 ft. to reach a belay below the start of Pinnacle Wall.

60 The Girdle of the Lower Amphitheatre Wall

ES— 475 ft. ** *James, Wilkinson, 1966.*
This very hard route traverses the lower wall taking in the crux of each route on the wall. The situations are superb whilst the abseil is most exciting.

Start at the foot of the Crack on the L. of the wall.

1 65 ft. Climb the Crack for 30 ft. until it is possible to step R. and so reach a good spike. Descend along a steep diagonal crack to reach the top of an overhang. Step across this and so pull onto a stance. High peg belay.

Plumbagin (HVS) reaches the overhang via the V chimney below and continues with a peg up the groove above and to the R.

2 100 ft. Descend and then traverse to reach a horizontal crack. Follow this until it is possible to step into a niche. Move round a corner into an adjacent niche (**Plate 17**). (Griseofulvin HVS reaches here from near the start of Mur Y Niwl and continues above.) Now semi hand traverse 30 ft. R. to near the arête (peg). Abseil 30 ft. free to the stance above pitch 2 of Mur Y Niwl.

3 70 ft. Pitch 3 of Mur Y Niwl. (Descend, traverse R. and then climb a diagonal crack to a perch).

4 70 ft. Descend the groove below the finger traverse, going down over a short overhang until a short traverse R. brings a jug on the arête within reach. With aid from a sling on this, descend to the beginning of a hand traverse, and follow this to a stance. (This hand traverse is part of Agrippa which comes up the wall below it.)

5 70 ft. Step down round the corner, then move up over two shelves to good holds leading up to a stance. (This is as for Agrippa).

6 50 ft. From the stance, move R. up the wall behind until it is possible to step across R. to a good foothold. Use a peg and sling to reach the final edge and so to a stance.

7 50 ft. Easily up the quartz slab to reach the Bilberry Terrace at its R. end.

Plate 18. The Diagonal Crack of Pinnacle Wall

61   Pinnacle Wall

S+ 235 ft. ** Kirkus, 1931.

Although not a very good line, this route gives a most enjoyable climb up the upper wall, with a fair feeling of exposure near the top.

Start at the R hand end of the Bilberry Terrace, below the end of the quartz ledge, at a stairway leading up R.

1   45 ft.   The rock staircase to a good stance.

2   90 ft.   Go up to 20 ft. to reach the quartz traverse. It is possible to walk across this, but usually a less dignified method feels far safer. A more awkward step at the end leads to a small stance and peg belay.

3   100 ft.   Climb up the corner above (a layback move helps here on the crux), then good holds in a diagonal crack (**Plate 18**) lead up to the top of the pinnacle. Step off this onto a final slab.

62   The Grimmett

VS. 155 ft. ** Cox, Beaumont, 1938.

Another good route, steep and direct, but very well protected, taking the overhanging wall to the L. of Pinnacle Wall.

Start above the L. hand end of the Bilberry Terrace, on the R. of a smaller terrace.

1   30 ft.   A steep corner crack leads to a cave below the first overhang.

2   75 ft.   Move out of the cave and continue up a groove above. A second bulge blocks this, so a swing L. and mantel-shelf (the crux) leads to a final overhang. Bridge this direct to reach grass and a stance up R.

3   50 ft.   Traverse back L. to reach good rough rock with excellent holds. Up this to more ledges. Two mantel-shelves above lead to the top.

Ogwen Area. Outlying Climbs

63   Chalkren Stairs. Gallt Yr Ogof

N. Facing Cliff. 1,250 ft. above sea-level. 220 ft. high. G.R. 692595.

This rather unattractive group of vegetated buttresses lies a few hundred yds. s. of the A5 road near Heyg It can be approached easily from the old road or via a bridge from the new road.

Parking at Williams' farm, Gwern y Gof Isaf. (GR 685601). Mountain rescue equipment and teams at Ogwen Cottage (GR 650603) and Plas Y Brenin (GR 716578).

Initially, the crag appears to be composed of two main sections separated by a diagonal rake which provides a descent route. Many odd routes take the slabs and buttresses well to the L. on the upper cliff, whilst an evil HVS +, Maria, climbs the central cave. To its R., one can find (?) four or five D to VD + routes. However, our route lies on the lower cliff and provides the best climbing on the cliff. This lower section is split by three gullies called respectively One Pitch, Green and Black for obvious reasons. To the L. of One Pitch lies a nice clean little buttress giving Three Pitch Buttress at D + standard whilst to the R. of it is a little bay with trees, etc. Further R., just L. of Black Gully, a steep wall gives three routes around s   standard.

   Start in the little bay.

1   **70 ft.**   Go up through trees and vegetation over occasional boiler plate slabs to a stance at the top near a steep wall.

2   **50 ft.**   Get into a steep V scoop on the R. with difficulty from the L. and continue up a groove above. Then climb a slab to a stance in a niche on the top L. side.

3   **30 ft.**   Go up L. to a ledge below an overhang. Traverse R. to a large stance and belays.

4   **20 ft.**   Go right round to the edge.

5   **50 ft.**   Climb the crack above.

64   Little Woodhead. Pinnacle Craig of Cwm Cywion

*VS. 240 ft. * Kirkus, Grosvenor, 1932.*
NE. Facing. 1,800 ft. above sea level. 200 ft. high.
G.R. 637602

This fine cliff is situated high on the shoulder of the NE. ridge of Y Garn. It is approached usually from Ogwen by going into Cwm Idwal, passing the experimental grazing plots, and so cutting round below the crag until an unpleasant scramble up the screes leads to its foot, or by traversing in from near Llyn Clyd. About 1 hr.

   Parking and mountain rescue facilities at Ogwen.

   The main features of the crag are the pinnacle and the gully which cuts it off from the main crag.

   Start about 10 yds. R. of the gully at the lowest point of the main buttress.

1   60 ft.   Take the quartzy wall to a grass ledge, then follow the arête above to grass and finally a steep groove with a spike to a stance on the R.

2   40 ft.   Climb the corner on the R.

3   30 ft.   Step with difficulty onto an exposed gangway and follow this to an exciting stance on perched blocks.

4   110 ft.   Go L., awkwardly, over a groove to reach an exposed but easy chimney. Up this to a ledge by a large block. Walk L. on this and go up easier slabs (grassy) to the top.

Pitch 2, the corner, is also the middle pitch of The Crack, another vs of interest, whilst the Pinnacle itself can be climbed by the crack up the face of it at vD+ standard. The walk to this crag is quite strenuous but the climbing is good and a descent by scree running quite fine.

65   Corrugated Cracks. The Pillar of Elidir

S. 180 ft. * Evans, Smith, 1937.
NE. Facing crag. 2,250 ft. above sea level. 200 ft. high.
G.R. 615616.

This isolated crag lies high on Elidir Fawr above Marchlyn Mawr. It can be approached via Foel Goch and so combined with the previous cliff, or a shorter walk can be made from near the new quarry above Mynydd Llandegai ($\frac{3}{4}$ hr.).

Parking at Ogwen or Mynydd Llandegai.

Mountain rescue facilities at Ogwen. Telephone at Mynydd Llandegai.

The main feature of the cliff is the gully (East Gully, D) which separates the Pillar from the main mass of the mountain. To its R. is a steep wall above the gully with a fine arête further R. which gives an enjoyable climb of D standard past an obvious curtain of rock. Two routes climb the wall between these lines; Mexico Cracks (HVS−) up a line of steep hard cracks starting 50 ft. up East Gully and the selected route climbing the wall just L. of the arête.

Start a little to the L. of the arête on a grass terrace.

1   90 ft.   Easy climbing to reach the foot of a prominent crack.

2   40 ft.   The narrow chimney above is difficult and strenuous until a pull over a chockstone leads into a wider section. Continue up this via a ledge on the L. until an awkward pull up leads on to a ledge.

3   50 ft.   Climb the easier chimney above facing R. until a crack on the R. leads to the top.

The final situation and the interest of the climbing should make the walk worthwhile. An excellent route for a Bank Holiday!

66   Western Gully. Ysgolion Duon (Black Ladders)

VD+ 950 ft. * **w** *Cooke, Brushfield, Owen, 1901.*
N. Facing crag. 2,400 ft. above sea level, 900 ft. high.
G.R. 668632.

This large cliff provides little good climbing, although it contains much impressive rock. It lies at the head of Cwm Llafar and can be reached by following the approach to Llech Ddu and continuing up to the valley head over unpleasant boulders for 20 mins. more.

Parking and mountain rescue facilities as for Llech Ddu.

The basic features of the face are simple; two prominent gullies, the L. hand being Central Gully (D+) and the R. hand Western Gully (VD+). L. of Central Gully a pyramid-shaped buttress which has the only other worthwhile climb, Jacob's Ladder (VD+) which takes as direct a line up this as the overhangs will allow. Western Gully gives an excellent gully climb on good steep rock. It can be very hard in winter conditions.

Start directly below the gully where the stream bed cuts deeply through the lower rocks to the screes.

1   80 ft.   Climb unpleasant grooves to grass in the gully bed, or climb easier rocks on the L. to utilise a little chimney.

2   180 ft.   Scramble up the gully past two small pitches.

3   70 ft.   Turn the first chockstone on the R. to more grass.

4   60 ft.   Fine climbing straight ahead.

5   60 ft.   Get up into the chimney (long runner on the R.) and climb it facing L. to reach a large stance.

6   30 ft.   Easily to a cave.

7   40 ft.   Exit R. past jammed stones to a stance below a groove.

8   70 ft.   The groove (difficult) to grass and vegetation above and finally a stance on the L.

9   35 ft.   Go easily L. until it is possible to climb the R. side of a jammed boulder to gain a large cave.

10   50 ft.   Step out R. and climb the slab (crux) to scree with a belay on the R.

11   65 ft.   A short scramble leads to a minor cirque from which a chimney on the L. provides the best exit.

12   35 ft.   Continue easily past (or through) the boulder bridge.

13   175 ft.   Scramble up to the ridge.

67   West Buttress. Craig LLoer

*S. 320 ft. * Kirkus, 1928.*
N. Facing crag. 2,600 ft. above sea level. 300 ft. high.
This steep crag lies above Ffynnon Lloer on the NE. side of Pen Yr Oleu-wen. It is reached easily by the path on the W. branch of the stream which enters Llyn Ogwen near Tal Y Llyn Ogwen farm.
40 mins.

Parking and rescue facilities as for Tryfan E. Face routes.

This crag has two buttresses and the route lies on the R. hand of these, which is seen in silhouette from the outflow of the lake.

Start just L. of some faint gullies at a cairn below a little chimney some 25 ft. L. of the toe of the buttress.

1   90 ft.   Climb the chimney and step out R. to reach a groove. Climb this for a few ft. until it is possible to make a traverse L. to the edge of a slab. Up this to a large stance.

2   60 ft.   An awkward rib leads to the foot of a steep crack. Thread runners. Climb the crack (crux) to finish on good holds.

3   30 ft.   Scramble up R. to heather, then an easy arête to a stance.

4   80 ft.   Move out R. delicately and try to follow the edge of the buttress. Bulges force one back L. to take the line of the easier square cut groove above the stance. However, persist on the R. to reach a slab and then a stance.

5   60 ft.   Up slabs above the belay, easing, to the top.

To descend, scramble higher until a steep little section leads down into the gully/amphitheatre on the L. The far wall of this gully presents a nice steep face with a variety of routes of which Hhier (VS), up grooves through a bubbly rock overhang in the centre of the wall is the best.

68 Cracked Arête. Carreg Mianog

*VS— 120 ft. * Ferguson, Williams, 1945.*
S. Facing. 1,650 ft. above sea level. 120 ft. high.
G.R. 686618.

This steep crag is situated at the end of the spur which runs down from point 3185 on Carnedd Dafydd, towards the farm of Glan Llugwy. It is easily approached from the farm (GR 684612) by taking the path out of the farmyard NE. to a bridge across the leat and then going direct to the cliff. 30 mins. from the main road.

Parking is discouraged at the farm, and so cars should be left on the roadside near a phone box. Mountain rescue facilities at Ogwen Cottage O.P.C.

The crag is in two sections, the W. Buttress on the L. and then after a grassy break, the E. Buttress. The route described lies up the central arête of the W. Buttress, crossing a horizontal break near the top. Other routes on the crag include an S+, Zip Wall, up the walls 10 yds. to the L. of the arête; a VD—, Crawl Climb, which zig-zags up the same area as the Cracked Arête and finally on the R. of this buttress a steep crack and the corner above, Crack and Corner Climb, VD. The R. hand buttress has three worthwhile routes, Biceps Wall (VS+) up the front, Funny Bone (VS+) and Knee Cap (HVS—) just on or round the nose. All the routes give steep climbing broken by horizontal ledges.

Start at the foot of the Arête, just above a small cave (Crawl Climb starts further R. on boulders below the cave).

1 80 ft. Step onto the bottom of the arête and climb it to a ledge just on the R. (runner). Now swing back L. to follow a delightful crack to reach a good ledge. (Crawl Climb creeps round here from R. to L.). Step up to the foot of a thin curving crack with good threads and nuts in it (crux) to arrive via a good handhold at a large ledge.

2 40 ft. As for Crawl Climb (which crept back in from the L.) up the corner crack.

B The Llanberis Pass

This is a deep cut valley enclosed by steep craggy slopes. The A4086 road follows it for 5 miles from Llanberis to Pen Y Pass through the small hamlet of Nant Peris. To the N. of the road lie the Glyders and all the climbing described on this side lies on low s. facing crags only a few hundred yds. from the road. However, to the s. lies the Snowdon massif, with numerous rock-walled cwms, and some of the finest crags in Britain. These are big cliffs with Clogwyn Du'r Arddu and Lliwedd giving the expert and/or the mountaineer great sport. Nearer the Pass, Dinas Mot provides many fine routes whilst Cyrn Las and the crags above in Cwm Glas add great variety to the climbs available.

The great range of climbs found in this area make it a delight for all standards and type of climber, although the easiest of routes are not as frequent as in Ogwen. Ferocity abounds, but amongst these very hard climbs can be found some superb VD's and s's. Protection is good except on the Nose of Dinas Mot.

In bad weather the cliffs on the N. of the Pass still give reasonable climbing and dry quickly, but the Mot and Lliwedd can be appreciably harder in the wet. In snow conditions, the gullies on Snowdon itself, in Cwm Glas and around Cloggy, all give pleasant sport, whilst the gullies and easier buttresses on Lliwedd and some of the old fashioned routes on Cloggy, plus Main Wall and the gullies on Cyrn Las give fine problems. Finally for the 'ice tigers' Black Cleft on Cloggy and the Waterfall Climb on Craig Rhaeadr have given two of the best modern winter ascents.

General Facilities

The pass provides the usual wide range of facilities as follows:

(i) Sleeping

Hotels at Pen Y Gwryd, and Llanberis.

Caravan park at Llanrug.

Guest houses at Nant Peris and Llanberis.

Farms with accommodation at Nant Peris.

Youth Hostels at Llanberis and Pen Y Pass.

Climbing huts:

Climbers Club at Ynys Ettws (624567) and Cwm Glas Cottage (619569).

Rucksack Club at Beudy Mawr (615575).

Chester Club at Llanberis.

Ceunant Club at Nant Peris (606583).

Camping sites at Llanberis, Nant Peris and near Pen Y Pass. Unofficial sites in the Pass (great care must be taken to avoid water pollution, wall damage and litter leaving if these are used). High camping below Cloggy, unofficially.

Bivouacing under boulders in the Pass, again requires great care and discretion.

Mountain centres at Llanberis, Glyn Padarn – Kent Education Authority; Bryn Refail – Hafod Meurig – Rainer Foundation.

(ii) Eating

Meals at hotels for non-residents. In Llanberis, Wendy's Cafe has become a centre for climbers to eat meals and snacks. Other cafes open seasonally, including a mobile hot dog stall in the Pass at the height of summer.

Food can be bought in Llanberis and Nant Peris. Early closing day Wednesday.

(iii) Drinking

There is a climbers' bar at Pen Y Gwyrd, usually very crowded, and others at Nant Peris and Llanberis, of which the Padarn Lake Hotel and the Dolbadarn Hotel seem to be the most popular at present.

(iv) Public Toilets

At Llanberis.

(v) Garages and Breakdown Facilities

Petrol station at Pen Y Gwryd. Garage with breakdown service at Llanberis (Davies, Llanberis 225).

(vi) Taxi and hire cars

Nearest at Capel Curig and Bangor (see Ogwen Valley).

(vii) Mountain Rescue

The official post for the area is at Pen Y Gwryd Hotel (660557) although often extra help is required from Plas Y Brenin or Llanberis Mountain Rescue Team (call out via Llanberis Police). In all cases of rescue ensure that Police H.Q. (dial 999) is informed. Rescue equipment also at Nant Peris.

(viii) Public 'Phone Boxes

These are located at Pen Y Gwryd and Nant Peris. Post offices at Nant Peris and Llanberis.

(ix) Climbing Equipment

This can be purchased at Joe Brown's shop in Llanberis.

Llanberis Pass. Dinas Y Gromlech. (Dinas Cromlech)

S. Facing. 1,400 ft. above sea-level. 150–350 ft. high. G.R. 629569. Plate 19.

Plate 19. Dinas Cromlech

This fine cliff lies above the Llanberis Pass, 600 ft. up the hillside from Pont Y Cromlech, and can be reached easily direct up the screes in about 20 mins.

Parking is possible at present in laybys in the pass, and also in a field by the bridge. In cases of need for mountain rescue aid, a message should be sent either to Pen Y Gwryd Hotel or to the Llanberis Rescue Team via the Llanberis Police.

The crag itself is composed, in the central section, of huge columns of rock forming square cut arêtes and corners. The sharpest of these corners is that of the Cenotaph, whilst the arête to its R. provides the improbable line of Cemetery Gates, and the next corner that of Ivy Sepulchre. To the R. of this central steep area lies a more broken area, giving routes of about s standard, whilst on the far R., an easier buttress abuts against the main cliff giving the delightful Flying Buttress climb. To the L. of the centre, walls and corners continue, but are smaller, giving various routes of s to vs plus one vd route well to the L. The numbers after the route names refer to **Plate 19.**

Generally, the climbing on the Cromlech is steep, on good holds and with excellent protection. Some of the rock is rather friable whilst many of the trees are nearing their last days. However, good footwork and balance pay great dividends on these routes and even the hard ones have been led by technically proficient ladies. For beginners, Flying Buttress provides an excellent introduction to steeper climbing.

69   Flying Buttress.   (8)
D. 320 ft. *** Edwards, 1931.

This is a delightful route following the R. side of the crag.

Start at the foot of the edge of the cliff below a broken subsidiary buttress. (All very well worn).

1   60 ft.   Climb the crest of the ridge by a groove, then easily by spillikins and finally by a steep little wall below a bulge to a good stance.

2   60 ft.   Continue up ribs, etc. on the crest to the final castellated edge of the subsidiary buttress. (**Plate 20**)

3   20 ft.   Descend over pinnacles to the gully bed. Belay below a tree which grows out of the rock wall.

Plate 20. At the top of pitch 2 on Flying Buttress

4 60 ft. Climb up past the tree, moving L. on rock steps, then traverse L., down and round onto the face, and up this diagonally by a crack to an exposed stance with giant belays.

5 70 ft. Step from the belays onto the wall above (awkward) and continue up this until forced R., round the corner to a ledge. Poor belays so continue up to a stance below the chimney.

6 50 ft. Climb the chimney (the crux) mainly on its R. to reach the top.

Descend from this route via a gully well to the R., out of which it is best to traverse R. at half height.

70 Ivy Sepulcre. (7)

*HVS— 220 ft. * Harding, 1947.*

The excellent climb follows the R. hand of the great corners on the crag and gives, on its main pitch, climbing of a sustained nature. Time, and many ascents, have removed the ivy and loose rock for which it was once famous, but nevertheless, it provides good climbing in a fine situation. One good protection piton is adequate and usual, although two or more appear from time to time.

Start directly below the corner on a grass ledge.

1 90 ft. Climb up L. to reach a crack and follow this until a traverse back R. leads to below a steeper area of rock. Climb this via two grooves to a good stance below the corner proper. It is best for the second to belay well out R. for communication in the upper part is difficult.

This first pitch is the start of Horseman Route (VS—) which continues low round the corner on the R. and then finishes up the steep corner just L. of Flying Buttress. The R. wall of Ivy Sepulchre is climbed by Jerico Wall, HVS and loose.

2 110 ft. Start the corner steeply by bridging until a very good hold on the L. wall can be reached. Use this to move up and into a small niche and leave this by leg jamming until a much larger niche is attained. Rest a little, then bridge up very wide to reach the crack above the roof (there is usually a peg on the R. wall for protection and often aid). Move up past this by semi layback (crux), to reach small finger-holds on the R. wall, and from these get better holds on the L., and so to a resting place. The wider crack ahead is climbed by strenuous leg jams, or by very wide bridging to reach easier angled rock. Continue up the open chimney ahead to reach a belay behind an oak tree.

3   20 ft.   Step out L. and so to the top.

Descent from here (the Valley) is possible by a variety of ways. Either go up the upper walls by routes between VS *and* ES —, *or by traversing* R. *and slightly down reach Flying Buttress at the end of pitch 4, and so up or down this. However, the best escape is via a walk* L. *(above the Corner) to reach a diagonal crack leading up* L. *to easy ground* (D —). *A walk then leads to the top of the crag and so down the usual way off.*

71   Cemetery Gates.   (6)

*HVS+ 170 ft. ** Brown and Whillans, 1951.*
This is one of the best hard routes in Wales, combining exposure, technical difficulty, small holds and interesting (but good) protection. The route climbs the arête between the Corner and Ivy Sepulchre, following mainly a crack on its L. side. Two pitons are usually in place for protection and a belay. although not essential.

Start by scrambling up to below the Corner, then walk out R. on to a detached flake. Chockstone belay below.

1   120 ft.   Climb down easily in a small chimney to reach the foot of the arête proper, and climb this on the R. on quite good holds, until a move L. brings one out onto the crest at a small overhung niche. One move up leads to a very big spike (good runner) and from this an open crack is reached, which is followed for 15 ft. to a holly stump. Resting place. Now pull up with difficulty to reach better holds, a slight ledge and a step L. to reach the main crack. Follow this for 30 ft. (good protection) to a niche where the crack almost vanishes (knee jamming rest). Swing out L. and move up (crux) to a slight niche and so reach a poor ledge; step R. to a stance (?), numerous line belays and sometimes a peg.

The Girdle Traverse (HVS+) crosses the R. wall to reach this stance and continues R. at this level to reach Ivy Sepulchre.

2   30 ft.   Climb the crack above the belays on undercut holds until good holds round the corner lead R. for 10 ft. to a break in the bulge and easier climbing to a grass ledge. Belay on L. above. (A strong leader will prefer to lead both these pitches in one to reach a good stance.)

3 20 ft. Easily up to the Valley. *Descent as for Ivy Sepulchre.*

72 Cenotaph Corner. (5)

HVS+ 120 ft. (150 ft. to a belay). *** *Brown, Belshaw, 1952.*

The pitch is one of the best in Britain, giving superb climbing in a perfect line up the centre of this fine cliff. A 'must' for all aspiring hard men, its ascent in good style makes an introduction to modern hard climbing. Two pitons are usually in place, more definitely are not needed, whilst a good leader will try to use less. Protection is good throughout, although a little cunning is needed to find it all!

Start directly below the Corner. A low piton is sensible as a belay.

1 120 ft. A few easy ft. lead to the foot, and fairly normal bridging follows to reach the first hard move by a good thread runner at 20 ft. Either swing out L. to reach jugs and a mantelshelf, or layback in the corner on finger-holds. The resting place above is followed by easier climbing at about vs mainly on the L. wall, until another resting place is reached where a ledge runs out onto the R. wall (**Plate 21**). (This is the stance of the Girdle Traverse!) The crack is now wider and some jamming moves lead to a large chockstone at about 90 ft. A second hard section follows into a niche with a piton and rest in a bridging position below the last few ft. This final section is hard and needs careful climbing to find a good finishing hold and so reach the top. Belay at a tree 20 ft. back.

Descent as for Ivy Sepulchre, Tributary Crack (D —) *is above on the L., or, of course, abseil to recover abandoned equipment!*

73 Spiral Stairs. (4)

D+ 280 ft. ** *Edwards, Darbishire, 1931.*

This route is the only easy way up this steep section of cliff, and even so requires steadiness and careful rope work, particularly by the last man in a party. Not ideal for complete novices. It finds an easy approach to the foot of the Corner and then escapes L. around two arêtes.

Plate 21. Half way on Cenotaph Corner

Plate 22. Carreg Wastad

Start on a grass ledge 90 ft. below the arête of Cemetery Gates.

1   100 ft.   Smooth rocks lead in steps to a narrow traversing path which is followed to below the L. wall of the Corner. Belays poor, a piton would help.

2   70 ft.   A short, very well worn crack leads up the wall for a few ft. to reach a traversing line and this is followed slightly downwards for about 50 ft. until a rib leads up to a stance below old trees, the Forest (Sabre Cut and Dives both visit this stance.)

3   70 ft.   Move up for a few ft. and then traverse L. again to reach a crack with a tree and use this to reach a ledge on the L. Climb up L. on good holds until easier slabs lead L. Spike belay and poor stance.

4   40 ft.   Climb a crack above the belay and then easy slabs to the top.

For the best descent, walk up to the top of the crag and so to the usual way down.

74   Sabre Cut.   (3)

*VS. 190 ft. * Pentir-Williams, Williams, 1935.*

The top pitch of this climb takes the well defined corner to the L. of Cenotaph Corner and goes straight up above the Forest. The remains of the Forest are reached from below on the L. Two good contrasting pitches.

Start at a vertical corner behind a rowan tree.

1   80 ft.   Bridge up the corner until it is possible, just below a small tree, to swing out onto the steep face on the R. Climb this on good holds to the Forest.

2   30 ft.   Scramble up through the Forest (as for Dives) until a stance can be taken on the very edge of the L. wall of Cenotaph Corner. Fine views! Epitaph (HVS+) goes up the arête from here, whilst the Girdle traverses out R. to reach the chock-stone artistry of the Left Wall Route (HVS) and then continues to the Corner.

3   80 ft.   Traverse into the crack on the L. and climb this past a good ledge with chock-stone runner, and then by bridging (or laybacking) to the top.

Scramble up and over the top for descent, or descend Spiral Stairs which finishes below and to the L.

75   Dives with Better Things finish.   (2)

*S. 220 ft. * Edwards, Davis, 1933.*

Interesting climbing to the L. of the start of Sabre

Cut and then finishing by the corner to its L.

Start 25 ft. L. of Sabre Cut, below a short, steep corner.

1 90 ft. Climb up easily to the foot of the corner and up this with difficulty to better holds and a ledge below the big black diagonal overhang. Traverse up R. on peculiar rock (sometimes wet) with a series of interesting moves to reach the Forest.

2 30 ft. Scramble up as for Sabre Cut to a stance on the edge.

3 100 ft. Traverse L. to below Sabre Cut and continue traversing to reach an arête. Move up this and then go round into a shallow corner. Climb this corner with difficulty (crux) for 30 ft. to reach an easier section. Belay here or continue to the top with less difficulty.

76 Pharoah's Wall. (1)

*VS. 200 ft. * Edwards, Hargreaves, 1933.*

The L. section of the cliff is composed of a series of walls and corners, nearly all of which give routes of quite an enjoyable nature. The exception is the farthest L. wall, black and overhanging, which gives a short, vicious ES— called The Thing. To its R. is a corner which gives a good VD+ (Parchment Passage) whilst the next corner, Pharoah's Passage, gives in its lower part a hard overhang (VS+) followed by an easy chimney (D—). However, the third corner and wall provide the best climbing on this section of cliff and is the route described here.

Start at the wall and corner about 90 ft. L. of Dives.

1 25 ft. Scramble up to below the smooth corner proper. Chock-stones.

2 85 ft. Climb diagonally out R. up the wall on small holds to reach a line of large pock marks and follow these direct around overhangs to a good stance and belays.

3 90 ft. Climb the steep wall above by the obvious chimney and then move out R. onto steeper rock. Up over a bulge via an overhanging flake and then difficult climbing until an escape R. is possible at the top.

A good descent from this section of the cliff is via the easy chimney a little to the L. and lower, and then an abseil. (Pharoah's Passage in reverse.)

Llanberis Pass. Carreg Wasted

S. Facing. 1,100 ft. above sea-level. 200–300 ft. high.
Plate 22. G.R. 626570.

This crag, the middle one of the Three Cliffs, lies a
few hundred yds. farther down the pass than the
Cromlech, directly opposite Ynys Ettws. It can be
reached easily from the road below in 10 mins., or
by traversing from the other crags.

Parking is possible at a small layby below Dinas
Cromlech and others below Clogwyn Y Grochen.
Rescue facilities as for the Cromlech.

The cliff itself is a boss of hard rock, flat topped,
which protrudes from the smoother hillsides around.
It has no gullies but four facets lying equally on
either side of the faint central depression, the line of
Erosion Groove. To the L. easier slabs lead in across
steeper rock to end at a steep, undercut nose (the
crux of Crackstone Rib) from which a wall leads into
the Groove. To the R., steep walls and overhangs
near the Groove merge into trees and less attractive
rock, finishing with a steep, red tower of very poor
rock on the far R.

Except for one pitch, the climbing on this cliff is
less vicious than on its two neighbours, with the two
easier routes being trade routes for the area. Some
care is needed with the rock.

77 Wrinkle

VD. 240 ft. * Ward, Barford, Pierre, 1947.
Nice climbing up the L. hand area of slabs.

Start at the L. of the crag, below and slightly L.
of some oak trees which are above a slight area of
overhang. Very well worn.

1 80 ft. Ziz-zag up the steep wall on excellent
holds to below some overhangs. (Skylon, vs−, continues above). Now traverse R. to reach a ledge and
follow this to the oak trees. Chockstone belays.

2 70 ft. Move low across R., behind the trees and
then step delicately R. to an earthy ledge. Follow
this easily to reach a grooved slab. Up this until
holds lead R. and another 10 ft. bring one to the top
of a small pedestal. Good belays.

3 90 ft. Step straight up and then L. until it is
possible to move back R. and so up the overlapping
grooved slabs to a ledge. Then easily up the broken
corner on the R. to the top. Belay well back.

Plate 23. On the rib of Crackstone Rib

Ways off this crag are easy via the gentle gullies on either side.

78 Unicorn

*HVS — 210 ft. * Harding, Rowland-Hodgkinson, Hughes, 1949.*

This is a fine route with a hard but safe crux. Most of the poor rock seems to have come off but some intelligence would be an asset on the top pitch.

Start at the lowest point of the crag, 60 ft. below a crack leading through a prominent overhang.

1 60 ft. Climb the reddish wall dodging difficulties to reach a few steeper moves on blocks. These lead to a comfortable stance below a groove which is just L. of the overhang. Lion vs+ starts here and goes out R. across a black wall, but is not very enjoyable above.

2 50 ft. Climb the groove with one peg (crux) to reach an easier crack above with holly trees and a secluded stance.

3 100 ft. Step up delicately R. to find a way out onto the rib on the R., then go up the side of this on small but adequate holds to reach easy ground.

Scrambling to the top or descend a corner on the R. to reach pitch 3 of Overlapping Wall Direct which provides a fitting final pitch.

79 Overlapping Wall Direct

*HVS — 260 ft. ** Hughes, 1948.*

This combination of steep pitches gives an excellent route which is well protected yet very open. Some finger strength or a long arm seems necessary.

Start 30 ft. R. of Unicorn, to the L. of a shallow, overhung grassy cave just before the crag starts to recede to the central depression.

1 100 ft. Climb up on the L. of the cave for 20 ft. until a traverse on good holds leads to a small ledge. Swing out L. and then up and back R. onto another ledge. Then via a groove to easier climbing and a big enclosed stance below a large chockstoned chimney.

2 70 ft. Climb the chimney until below the chockstone, then swing out L. onto a rib (resting place). Climb the overhanging bulge above on fingerholds (crux) and then traverse L. for a few ft. until a groove leads back R. to reach a ledge. Walk across the ledge to belays in the corner.

3 90 ft. Traverse out R. onto the nose and climb this on good holds to reach the top block of Crackstone Rib.

Plate 24. *At the piton on Ribstone Crack in nailed boots. Erosion Groove just to the R.*

80 Crackstone Rib

*S. 180 ft. ** Edwards, Joyce, 1935.*

One of the classic climbs of the area, this route gives delightful, airy climbing up the crest of the rib which forms the limit of the first facet of the crag.

Start below the central depression and a little to the L.

1 30 ft. Climb easily up to a groove which leads to a flat ledge. Belay on L.

2 80 ft. Traverse L. out towards the nose to a depression before the edge, good runners or a poor stance possible. Then step boldly round onto the rib and go up this delicately (**Plate 23**) with one hard move near the top. From a ledge, move up on good hand holds to reach a better ledge and a selection of belays.

3 70 ft. Step up slightly and then traverse into a slight corner. Climb this past an old tree stump to reach two traverse lines going L. The lower is easier but a good runner can be arranged to protect the upper one. Either way, reach a worn finger crack which after a hard step gives easier climbing to blocks and a tree.

81 Ribstone Crack

*VS. 160 ft. * Disley and Moulam, 1951.*

This fine route takes a direct line up the wall above the start of Crackstone Rib, using a crack about 20 ft. out from the main corner.

Start below the crack as for Crackstone Rib.

1 30 ft. Easily up to a little groove. Belays on the L.

2 80 ft. Step out R. and move up to below a small chimney. Avoid this by a few moves on the R. and then a dainty traverse back into the crack by a good runner. Interesting moves continue up the crack line until a small resting place is reached at 50 ft. (Runners). Now move up delicately on finger holds and finger jams to reach a piton (**Plate 24**) and, with protection and some aid from this, attain a bridging position. Finally a few delicate steps lead to an open groove and so to a stance just over the edge from Crackstone Rib.

3 50 ft. Step R. and then up to a flake crack. Go up this and mantel-shelf out onto the top of the flake. Then up L. and so to the top.

82   Erosion Groove Direct

ES — 180 ft. * *Whillans, others, 1953/55.*

This desperate route takes the main depression in its
middle part and then finishes up an extremely hard
open groove in the R. wall. One piton is usual on
pitch 2 which merits a HVS— grade, whilst the top
pitch is done clean when it is done at all.

Start below and to the R. of the central depression,
where a tree filled crack leads to the top of a large
flake.

1   50 ft.   Scramble up to the crack and step L. into
it. Up this to a sitting stance on the flake.

2   65 ft.   Step across into the corner and go up this
after using holds on the steeper R. wall. At a small
overhang at 45 ft., a piton on the L. gives aid and
allows the final overhang to be reached. This usually
is taken facing L. in an odd, layback type position.
(It is now possible to continue up the corner without
great difficulty.)

3   65 ft.   Step R. from the stance to reach a flake
with under-cut holds. By laying away on these and
utilising small footholds on the wall, movement is
possible, sometimes upwards. Continue in this line,
which eases to become a groove, to below a final
overhang. Provided some strength has been pre-
served, this is not as difficult as the lower section.

83   Shadow Wall

VS — 140 ft. * *Edwards, Joyce, 1935.*

One of the best routes of this standard in the valley
with the crux in a fine position. The bad rock which
used to exist has disappeared almost completely.

Start directly below the great diagonal overhang
which lies just to the R. of the central depression and
a few ft. R. of the Erosion Groove start.

1   80 ft.   Climb the groove to a good stance by a
holly tree, then continue in a more open position to
reach a stance below the great roof. Either chockstone belay in the corner (cramped) or spikes out on
the L. arête (better view but precarious).

2   40 ft.   An exposed upwards traverse joins the
three ledges below the roof. Security can be improved
by keeping one arm in the crack until the last ledge
is reached (chockstone runner). Now, for the crux,
a variety of possibilities exist. Either continue high
using the roof crack (hard), or swing R. and then
mantel-shelf (interesting), or swing R. round the

Plate 25. Nea Morin on the crux of Nea. Hidden ledge of Phantom Rib to her L.

corner keeping low (safest). Anyway, cross a rib to reach trees in a groove and stances (to protect seconds and observe their antics, the highest stance is best).

Trilon (vs−) reaches this point from directly below, up the rib. It starts in a cluster of yew trees and reaches the rib via a traverse and a piton move near a large overhang.

3   20 ft.   Straight up just L. of the trees to the top.

84   Bole Way Direct
VS+ 285 ft. Moulam, Pigott, Hyde, 1951.
This route makes the best of the rock on the R.-hand part of the cliff, which is generally more vegetated and less firm than the other sections. It takes a fairly direct line up a series of grooves and cracks which cut the area of cleaner rock just R. of a high, under-cut nose. Start at the foot of twin grooves, 10 yds. L. of a ramp which leads R. to a chimney.

1   90 ft.   Up the groove until the central rib can be used, runner at the top. Now a wide step across R. to reach an awkward diagonal rake and up this until better holds lead straight up to a nest above.

2   40 ft.   Up behind the trees to reach grooved slabs leading L. Up these delicately to reach a good tree stance below a steep groove (the First Bole).

3   35 ft.   Climb the groove above (some poor rock) to reach more trees (the Second Bole).

4   70 ft.   Climb up using trees to below the roof, then swing out R. onto a very open ledge (the con-trast from the enclosure of the trees is sensational), and follow this R. (peg) to reach a better ledge and a small stance with difficult belays.

5   50 ft.   Traverse back L. onto the crest and go up a very exposed crack on jams (crux) moving a little L. to the top.

Llanberis Pass. Clogwyn Y Grochan
S. Facing. 700 ft. above sea level. 300 ft. high.
G.R. 621572.

This is the lowest of the Three Cliffs, lying a short way from the road a few hundred yds. below Ynys Ettws. It can be reached from the road in a few mins. or from Carreg Wastad by a gentle descending traverse.

Parking is possible at present in laybys below the cliffs although in summer these are so full with

spectators that performers can have problems.
Rescue facilities as for the Cromlech.

The predominant features of the crag are the two horrid gullies which subdivide it (Goat's Gully on the L. and Central Gully on the R.), and the noticeable change in angle from the lower vertical walls to the upper, still steep walls of softer rock. The L. hand buttress, containing the first three routes, is called Goat's Buttress and has good rock almost to the top. The central area has very steep lower walls giving many excellent pitches of which four are described, whilst its upper part is much inferior, so that only the upper section of Brant is included. Finally the R. hand buttress is less pleasant, giving, in general, routes on poor rock of which only the s Scrambler's Gate is included.

The climbing on this cliff is, in general, fiercer than on its two companions.

Above and to the L. of the crag lies a smaller crag of excellent rock, Drws Y Gwynt, which makes a fine addition to any of the lower routes, giving two fine climbs, Little Sepulchre (vs —) up the obvious corner by layback or jamming and Cracked Wall, a delightful VD — of 100 ft. up the rough cracks and walls on the R. of the corner.

85   Nea

S. 235 ft. *** Mme Morin, Edward, 1941.
This popular route follows the long, diagonal crack which splits Goat's Buttress. It provides a good introduction to the type of climbing found on the crag.

Start on a big ledge a few ft. up the cliff, below a corner, and reached by a short scramble from the L.

1   70 ft.   Climb up behind the tree in the corner and follow its L. branch to a steeper section. From a bridged position (good nut runner), step delicately R. round the rib (crux) (**Plate 25**) and so to a crack and in 10 ft. a poor stance at the remnants of a holly tree. Good chockstone belays.

2   75 ft.   Follow the corner crack, now slabbier, past an awkward step to reach ledges and a belay on pinnacles.

3   40 ft.   A steep, yellow corner goes up the wall and this is followed with a high move to reach another ledge.

4   50 ft.   Now easier climbing above to reach top.

Descent from the top of this cliff is quite difficult and needs care. The ledge at the top of Nea is 50 ft. below the top and those descending from other routes must reach it either direct via two grassy traverses, or via a chimney (awkward) above its L. end. The top of the chimney is seen easily via a finger stone, but the grass traverses are easier. All of this leads to the gully on the L. of the cliff and this is descended with excursions onto the cliff. It is M standard and sometimes quite greasy.

86 Phantom Rib

VS. 260 ft. * Pigott, Miss Kennedy-Frazer, Stook.
This delightful route takes the crest of the rib on Goat's Buttress L. of Nea. Good footwork and balance, or very strong fingers seem essential. It needs cunning to protect the crux.

Start on the ledge below Nea, low on its L. side.
1 40 ft. Step down L. from the ledge to reach twin cracks with trees. Up these to reach an earthy stance level with a triangular overhang. Hazel Groove (s+) reaches this stance from Nea and continues straight up above via grooves and cracks.
2 40 ft. Climb the small groove behind the stance and then traverse out onto the R. wall, keeping low until a 'surprise' hold on the nose enables a good move to be made onto a ledge on the nose visible on **Plate 25**. Resting place. Now move very delicately up the rib on finger holds and finally continue on the R. on better holds. Good belays in a corner above R.
3 60 ft. Do not go up into the trees (although it is tempting) but climb diagonally R-wards up a series of small grooves in a yellow wall. At the highest of these, step blindly R. around the corner to another groove. Finger jams in this lead to blocks and a stance.
4 60 ft. Traverse R. until holds lead up and another ledge goes back L. Difficulties now ease and another stance, much better than the last, is reached. Some leaders, no doubt, will omit the previous stance to the anguish of their seconds.
5 60 ft. Easily up R. to an oak tree. Then further R. to join the last few ft. of Nea.

87 Spectre

HVS− 300 ft. ** Harding, Phillips, 1947.
This fine route takes a line up the centre of the nose below the fault of Nea, but with the final pitch to the L. of Nea. The two main pitches are excellent

and the second of these may be found to be harder than the standard suggests, success being very dependent on one's own particular style of climbing.

Start at lowest point of Goat's Buttress.

1 65 ft. A well worn, thin crack, very hard to start, leads up to better holds on a traverse R. just under the Nea starting ledge, and so on up easier rock to below the main crack line. Stance in trees. A good place for second thoughts, for the next pitch is harder.

2 70 ft. Climb straight up the crack to a ledge with a piton runner. Now swing out L. to reach a slab (?) with small holds. Go up across this L. to reach a groove, which leads with less difficulty to a stance and belay.

3 30 ft. An easy traverse across the slabs to reach the foot of an obvious crack. (Nea can be reached by a traverse in the opposite direction!)

4 30 ft. The crack is entered by a suitable method. Layback for the bold, mantel-shelf for the gymnast, or belly roll and leg kicking for the masses. Once entered, the trap is sprung, for retreat is virtually impossible and the exit is extremely hard. Hand jamming and foot scraping seem the usual technique required to reach a fine stance just below the Nea pinnacles.

5 65 ft. Cross Nea and traverse out low across the L. wall until a groove leads up with quite good holds.

6 40 ft. As for Nea or Phantom Rib.

88 Sickle

*HVS. 220 ft. * Brown, Cowan, 1953.*

This hard route takes the best line up the steep lower walls of the central area near Goat's Gully. The finish described crosses the gully in its upper part, to finish on Spectre or Nea.

Start a few ft. L. of an obvious 90 ft. corner (Brant Direct Start) at the L. hand side of a great flake, and below smooth walls and overhangs.

1 70 ft. Climb the steep crack on good holds to the top of the flake. After fixing a large runner, step out L. onto the wall and follow the thin crack to better holds and a ledge. Move up into a niche (old peg) and then step R. round a bulge and so up to a slanting stance. Peg belays.

2 60 ft. Move up a little to a thread runner and then step down L. to reach a line of holds (hands in

Plate 26. Brant – first pitch

a slot and feet on ledges, but all very steep) until a move can be made round a corner into a groove. Up this to better holds and a resting place. Now move delicately out L. to pockets above the overhang and so up slabs, sometimes wet, to a good stance. Nuts or peg belay.

3   90 ft.   Climb diagonally L. across pleasant slabs to the gully and then reach a steep crack in its L. wall which leads to the stance above pitch 4 of Spectre.

Either continue up Spectre, or up or down Nea. The latter gives the best combination (but only on a quiet day!)

89   Brant

VS. 360 ft. *** Edwards, Barford, 1940.

The classic route of the early era on these cliffs, taking the easiest line up the lower walls and the best up the upper section.

Start about 80 ft. R. of Brant Direct start, on the top of a pile of blocks.

1   45 ft.   Climb up towards a niche and make a hard traverse L. (crux) to reach a good hold and so to easier climbing (**Plate 26**) up L. a little, then by a crack R. to a stance in trees.

2   25 ft.   Climb over a flake and continue easily L. to a crevassed stance by a tree. (Slape, a similar route to Brant, climbs the wall above.)

3   50 ft.   Continue L. to the top of the Direct start (HVS−) and duck round a corner to reach a small V-chimney. Many techniques have been used to ascend this section but the easiest is to avoid it by stepping out onto the L. rib almost at once, whilst the hardest seems to be bridging facing out! Good nuts all the way make a conventional ascent quite safe. Now continue up an easy ledge R. to a superb stance.

4   80 ft.   Make an ascending traverse L. to reach the upper slabs which give more difficulty than would be expected. First go straight up to a nose and step onto this from the R. Then continue until it is possible to get to a small stance in a corner on the R. Nut belays.

5   70 ft.   Climb the corner for about 50 ft. and step out to reach easier climbing leading to a large yew tree.

6   90 ft.   Continue straight up past a red bulge to

reach easy rocks and a groove leading to the top cliff.

90   Surplomb

ES— 135 ft. ** *Brown and Williams, 1953.*

This is the hardest route on the cliff and gives a very difficult climb. Technically trying, it is also strenuous and not over endowed with protection. It has been climbed clean although one sling for aid is a usual (very meagre) minimum.

Start as for Brant.

1   40 ft.   Get into the first niche of Brant and then step out R. (sling for aid if you can find the right spike) to reach a line of holds leading up R. They are good but spaced and require bold, strong climbing. A piton belay is sometimes used but should be removed as this stance is on the traverse of Slape.

2   45 ft.   The chimney above is climbed by backing and jamming. Very tiring.

3   50 ft.   Bridge up the chimney until a very bold move can be made onto the L. arête (crux) and this climbed on small holds to a slight ledge. Step L. and then climb an appropriately shattered crack.

The difficulties are now over and a leader who has got this far will, no doubt, be able to escape from the cliff. However, if darkness is nigh, the best course is to traverse about 40 ft. R. until an abseil is possible from some trees as for Kaisergebirge Wall.

91   Kaisergebirge Wall

HVS— 120 ft. * *Harding, Disley, Moulam, 1948.*

This fine route takes a diagonal line up the wall to the L. of Central Gully. Between Brant start and this route lies a steep line of grooves which gives the line of Hangover (HVS+), except for one section when it uses the wall on the R. Slape (VS) also starts up these grooves but leaves them almost immediately for an interesting traverse L. across Surplomb.

Start 40 ft. from the gully at an obvious traverse line.

1   100 ft.   Traverse L. with increasing difficulty (one very awkward step up) to reach ledges leading L. Just before the shallow groove which gives the crux, running belays should be arranged in a thin crack. The groove is very hard for about 15 ft., whilst the final section is still very steep. Good stance and holly belays. *Either abseil from here*, or

2   20 ft.   Climb up the wall on the R. to reach

grass fields (Lords) and *across these to a tree and abseil to the gully.*

92   Scrambler's Gate
S. 215 ft. Edwards, Noyce, 1935.
Most of the rock immediately R. of Central Gully is very steep and loose. N'Gombo (HVS) takes this wall, whilst Ocre Groove (HVS−) follows grooves on the edge of this area. However, further R. the rock is better and this pleasant route finds the easiest way up it.

Start at an easy chimney facing down the pass, just R. of an obvious corner, usually wet (Broad Walk, VS+).

1   70 ft.   Up the chimney and after a short walk R., climb a small wall to a stance amongst trees (The Garden).

2   35 ft.   Walk and scramble L. to a rock stance on the edge of Broad Walk.

3   40 ft.   Descend a few ft., cross Broad Walk and continue to reach good holds near a crack leading up to a sloping ledge.

4   70 ft.   Step round L. to a rake and then go straight up delicately, to reach blocks and an oak tree (stance). Climb up behind the oak to a small groove and up this R. (crux) to ledges and grass.

Scrambling remains to the top of the cliff. From here, Drws Y Gwynt GR 621573 can be seen well over to the L. and provides an interesting addition to the day's climbing.

Llanberis Pass. Craig Ddu
S. Facing. 700 ft. above sea-level. 250 ft. high.
G.R. 618573.
This is the final cliff on the N. side of the Pass, and is easily recognized by its wet, black appearance. It is best approached from the road below Clogwyn Y Grochan by a diagonal walk in a few mins.

Parking and rescue facilities as for the Grochan.

The only real feature of the crag is a wet, diagonal gully, Garlic Groove (S) which divides the main L. part of the crag from the slab-topped R. section. On the main section, an obvious chimney with a large tree above it gives the line of Short Tree Chimney, a D on the far L., whilst a large pinnacle marks the line of Black Wall. This is the only route included in this section, although Canol (HVS+) gives an excellent pitch up the steepest part of the walls to the L. of the pinnacle. The R. hand section of the crag contains two good routes, Anthropology and Yellow Groove, whilst the edge of the buttress nearest Garlic Groove gives an obvious VD−, Rib and Slab.

In general, the climbing on this cliff is hard, particularly as the cliff takes a long time to dry. However, when it is dry, it gives some excellent routes.

93 Black Wall
*HVS. 210 ft. ** Whillans, Brown, 1954.*
This climb takes a line up the cliff above the large pinnacle and provides sustained hard climbing.

Start at the foot of the pinnacle, below a wide crack.

1 45 ft. Traverse out onto the L. arête and climb this to the top of the pinnacle. (Scrog, HVS, climbs the wide crack and continues up a line of cracks on R.)

2 50 ft. Go up the wall on the L. and then traverse L. to a good stance below an overhanging crack.

3 80 ft. Bridge up the overhang and then swing out L. onto good holds. Continue direct for 15 ft. until it is possible to step R. to a thin crack. Up this with a peg for aid, then a shallow groove on the L. leads to an awkward niche under the roof. Traverse diagonally L. across a slab to reach a good stance and belays.

4 35 ft. Continue up easier rocks to the grassy top of the crag.

Descent from this route is best made by a long traverse L. down steep grass until easier slopes lead back to the foot.

94 Anthropology
*VS. 200 ft. * Edwards, Davies, Monkhouse, 1949.*
This most enjoyable route takes the diagonal slabs and overhanging crack which cut across the face of the R. hand section of the crag.

Start 10 yds. R. of the dry stone wall which meets the crag below the easier upper slabs.

1 70 ft. Easily up the wall on good holds to a runner, then an ascending traverse R. on much steeper rock enables the lower slab to be reached. This is climbed to a stance and belay below the overhanging crack.

2 90 ft. The crack (crux) is climbed on interesting holds (and often a peg!) to reach the next layer of slab, and this climbed to reach a stance on the top

Plate 27. Clogwyn Du'r Arddu

of a pedestal from whence the cries of the second are inaudible!

3 40 ft. Climb L. up to a groove and leave this by exposed climbing on weird holds on the L. arête to the top.

Descent from this and the following route is best via Rib and Slab which finishes a few ft. to the L.

95 Yellow Groove
*VS. 150 ft. * Brown, Whillans, 1955.*

The top pitch of this route gives superb climbing up very steep rock on good holds.

Start at the top of grass pyramid, higher than, and well to the R. of Anthropology, below a yellow wall. It can be approached as easily from the R. as from the L.

1 50 ft. Easily up a gentle rock cone to a block.

2 100 ft. Climb the groove above the block for 10 ft. to a roof and then step R. to a ledge below a clean groove. Climb this on good holds to a smaller ledge and then go up delicately the wall above (crux) to finish on grass.

Snowdon. Clogwyn Du'r Arddu
N. Facing. 2,300 ft. above sea-level. 600 ft. high.
G.R. 6055. Plate 27.

This cliff, one of the best in Britain, lies high on the N. flanks of Snowdon, above the little lake of Llyn Du'r Arddu. It is reached best from Llanberis town by following a narrow road (close the gates!) which starts a few yds. above the Mountain Railway Station. Leave the road and join the Llanberis Path to Snowdon summit at a convenient place. This path is followed until, a few hundred yds. above Halfway House, a traversing path goes round the cwm to the crag. Usually an hr. from the cars including a stop.

Some parking is possible in laybys on the narrow road.

In case of accidents, a message should be sent to Llanberis Police giving very accurate details of the situation, particularly with reference to the injuries of the climber and his exact position on the crag.

Cloggy is a complex cliff of seven buttresses containing nearly a hundred routes. The majority of the routes are good, and nearly all are hard, including

some of the hardest in the country. The rather
meagre selection included here serves only as an
introduction to the crag, and is intended to give a
general impression of the climbing on the cliff. They
do include, however, some of the best climbs on it,
and a visitor who managed these nineteen routes in a
fortnight could go home well pleased with his efforts.

All but one of the routes lie on the three main
sections of the crag. The first six lie on the East
Buttress, a steep, smooth area of walls divided by
cracks, the foot of which the footpath meets first.
Then come five on the Pinnacle, a two-faced tower
which lies immediately above the East Buttress, and
is so impressive when seen on the approach walk.
Then follows seven routes on the less steep West
Buttress, a great area of overlapping slabs and corners
to the R. of the central fault. Finally, one route, The
Mostest, can be found on the Far East Buttress, a
sheer tower, very high and well to the L. of the rest
of the crag, which is best reached from above by
following the path to within 10 mins. of Snowdon
summit and then traversing. Of the other sections of
the crag, the Far Far East Buttress lies below and
to the L. of the Mostest and contains only one route;
Middle Rock lies below the central fault and has
short routes, usually around vs, whilst the Far West
Buttress is the great area of less steep slab lying
below and to the R. of the West Buttress giving
routes of D and VD standard with one hard route
up the steep L. hand band. Numbers following the
names of routes refer to **Plate 27.**

In general, the climbing on this cliff is serious, and
in poor weather it can become very hard indeed.
Holds are good but some rock is rather friable, and
so chocks and nuts give better protection than slings
on spikes. Good technique pays dividends on this
cliff and so Cloggy is a place to exercise ones skills,
not learn them. Finally, it is worth noting that many
recent accidents on the cliff on busy days have been
caused by falling rocks, so that crash hats are a must!

96   Llithrig. (1)
*HVS. 250 ft. ** Brown, Allan, 1952.*
After the traverse round the cwm, the path passes
below an obvious gully (East Gully) and goes up
over a little scree cone to come below the East
Buttress. The first feature to be seen on the buttress

is a long, E. facing crack, Sunset Crack (vs), and our route starts in this but then breaks out R. across smooth walls to finish up a faint groove. The route is well sustained at its standard and gives excellent climbing and interesting rope work.

Start on grass ledges a few ft. above the path, below the crack.

1 50 ft. Climb up to the L. a little and then traverse back across to a good stance below the crack proper.

2 70 ft. Step out R. quite low across to a steep groove, and go up this and the arête on its R. to a well worn place where pegs have been. Ignoring the groove directly above (Serth, ES−), step down below the overhang and move round it on the R. with difficulty. Better holds arrive (or you go to meet them!) leading diagonally up to a pair of spike runners. Leaving a short sling on the higher, and a runner on the lower, make a semi-abseil diagonally to a break on the R., and climb this to a fine ledge and peg belays. If intelligent rope work is used, the sling can be flicked off after the second is across.

3 70 ft. Step R. to the foot of an open groove and go up this with less difficulty for a few ft., good runners, and then move L. into a steeper crack which gives harder climbing until a sudden escape can be made L. to an easier line and a stance and belays.

4 40 ft. Leave the stance by a very awkward pull onto a good ledge. Step up and then traverse delicately L. to reach a shallow crack and go up this a little until escape is possible once again out L.

5 20 ft. Easily up the cracks behind to reach Green Gallery, a large, steeply sloping grass terrace below the Pinnacle.

Way off to the R. and upwards to reach a great sloping scree terrace, Eastern Terrace, but it is more fitting to do Octo (104).

97 Pigott's Climb. (2)
VS+ 270 ft. *** **w** *Pigott, others, 1927.*

This great classic follows the next break in the buttress, up a series of giant steps cut by corner cracks. It seems bigger than it is, with some quite strenuous pitches. In bad weather, or in winter, it gives a very hard day.

Start at a mossy spring on the path.

1 60 ft. Climb L-wards up a series of ledges to

reach a very awkward groove. Stance and good belays at the top.

2 50 ft. Go up easily from the R. of the stance and so reach a traverse which leads to a small 10 ft. corner. This is very hard and is best climbed facing L. to arrive, sitting, on the next stance. (The Conservatory).

3 70 ft. Easier climbing (and enclosed) up first the corner, and then a chimney on the R. to the top of a rock tower.

4 60 ft. The crux pitch (although a leader who works hard for this one may find the next even harder). The corner crack is climbed by bridging and jamming (chockstones usually give protection) until a move R. is possible to below a small, cracked overhang. Over this to another good stance.

5 30 ft. Many alternatives exist to the R. and even round the corner, but it is best to continue up the corner crack (spike runner at 20 ft.) to arrive at the Green Gallery.

Scramble off to the R. for no suitable finish up the Pinnacle is described here, although the Direct Finish to the East Buttress takes the crack tucked away round the R hand side of the Pinnacle, and is only VS.

98 Vember. (4)
*HVS+ 310 ft. ** Brown, Whillans, 1951.*
After the steep cracks and steps of Pigott's Climb, comes a rather uninspiring wall and then a deep crack (Chimney Route VS−) which gives pleasant climbing and a sharp little overhang for a crux. On its R. wall, a thin crack and higher, an open groove, give the line of Diglyph HVS, a route in the Llithrig class, but less sustained, although the crux about 90 ft. up needs a peg, and often a sling as well. Diglyph has a line of incipient grooves to its R., which mark the edge of a large expanse of very steep, smooth rock, the 200 ft. Great Wall (ES). The climbing of this, by a line of faint cracks and grooves on its L. side, using three pegs and five slings, gives one of the hardest routes in Britain. The R. hand side of this wall is marked by a steep crack which forks at half-height and it is this which gives the start of Vember, one of the best routes on the cliff. It gives fine open climbing with excellent protection.

Start at the foot of the crack.

Plate 28. Curving Crack. The classic layback start

1   **110 ft.**   From a small pedestal, climb the
crack, the first 20 ft. being hard and poorly protected.
Bold laybacking is best for soon things improve,
runners appear and jamming and bridging are
possible until, at 90 ft., a grass rake is reached, and
the R. fork of the crack reached at a stance on the
R. (The L. fork gives November, HVS + with the aid
of 4 slings on chockstones.)

2   **120 ft.**   Climb a short corner to a small ledge
and then continue to a groove which overhangs
(crux) until better holds lead up to a peg runner.
Above L. an open chimney, and cracks lead up to a
large grass terrace (The Lawn).

3   **80 ft.**   A crack at the back, and easier climbing
up walls lead to Eastern Terrace.

99 Curving Crack

VS. 200 ft. * **w** *Kirkus, others, 1932.*
Another classic route taking the obvious curving
groove to the R. of Vember. However, it is reached
from the R. by its hardest pitch. A good introduction
to the East Buttress.

Start at the top of an easy angled slab, below a
pillar which starts below the curving groove. A
corner crack.

1   **35 ft.**   The crux. Climb the crack by jambing
or laybacking. Good runner half way (**Plate 28**).
Stance at the top of the pillar. (A hard route, Troach
ES −, goes R., up the wall from here, with a sling and
two pegs for aid.)

2   **50 ft.**   Step down L. around a corner into the
groove proper, and after a few ft. on good holds, a
harder move brings the easier angled middle section
into reach. Continue up this until a good stance
appears on the L. wall.

3   **70 ft.**   Traverse back into the corner and up
this until easier climbing is possible on the R. wall.
Up this to a good stance.

4   **45 ft.**   Move out onto the arête, and on good
holds, although exposed, continue to the top.

100   Pedestal Crack. (5)

VS. 190 ft. * *Kirkus, MacPhee, 1931.*
Although quite short, this route gives some excellent
open crack climbing reaching the next fault on the

R. of Curving Crack via the large pedestal below it.
    Start a few ft. R. of Curving Crack at a grass ledge
below the pedestal.
1   **60 ft.**   Do not climb the steep corner crack
(Direct Start HVS−) but step out onto the nose on
the R. and go up this until easier climbing leads R.
and so to the top of the pedestal. (Scorpio, ES−,
takes the wall to the R. of this stance, using a peg.)
2   **30 ft.**   The first 20 ft. of the main crack above
provides the crux, laying away giving the answer, to
bring a small stance within reach.
3   **100 ft.**   Steep bridging up the crack for 40 ft.,
and then easier climbing direct to grass and the top.

101   The Corner
HVS. 190 ft. * Brown, Allen, Belshaw, 1952.
This good pitch takes the last major fault line on the
East Buttress, and lies above the end of the horizontal
section of the path below the crag.
Start on the path directly below the corner, although
often the first pitch is omitted, and the route reached
by the first pitch of Pedestal Crack and a grass
traverse.
1   **70 ft.**   Up grass ledges to a crack, then L. to
more grass and the corner proper.
2   **120 ft.**   Climb the corner easily at first, then go
onto the L. wall, up it a little, then back into the
corner. It is hard for the next section, involving L.
arm and leg work. Soon a subsidiary crack appears
on the R. wall and it eases, although still giving good
VS to the top. Peg belay on the Eastern Terrace.

102   Shrike
HVS+ 190 ft. *** Brown, Smith, Smith, 1958.
The Pinnacle lies above the East Buttress, and
presents two obvious facets. The first lies at right-
angles to the face of the East Buttress, and so gets
the morning sun in summer; this face rises out of the
East Gully, a rather loose opening on the L. of the
East Buttress. This superb route takes the highest
walls of this face, starting high up the Gully and can
be reached either by ascending the Gully or by
descending, by abseil, from its upper part, which
lies on the L. of this wall.
    Start 150 ft. R. of the top section of the Gully, in
a corner, below overhangs. A 20 ft. pinnacle leans
against the wall.

Plate 29. Shrike, Pitch 2 pulling round the overhang

1　**70 ft.**　Climb the crack on the L. of the pinnacle for a few ft. (hard), and then traverse horizontally L. on good holds to below a piton. Reach this, and using it for direct aid, move out L. to better holds, and up to a small, sitting stance and peg belay. (East Gully Wall, HVS, starts up here and then continues L. around a corner to reach a crack, which it follows to the top.)

2　**120 ft.**　Go straight up above the stance to a good piton, and using this, and two slings for aid, climb the overhang and the thin crack above it (**Plate 29**). The crack now widens unpleasantly, so traverse out on goods holds to near the arête, move up and then traverse back to the crack. A series of hard moves lead past two good spikes to a ledge on the R. which gives a welcome resting place. Move back L. past a loose looking flake to reach the arête and good runners. Step back R. to an out-of-balance ledge, and a final, awkward 10 ft. wall to reach the top, a fine jughandle hold. Peg belay. Careful separating of a double rope will allow excellent protection on this pitch, hence the pleasures of the route can be enjoyed without too much mental stress.

103　East Gully Groove

VS+ 160 ft. * **w** *Whillans, Allen, 1953.*
This is the most reasonable route up the faces of the Pinnacle, but still involves very steep climbing in places on poor rock. It can be very well protected.

Start a few ft. R. of Shrike, up the crack on the R. of the 20 ft. pinnacle.

1　**20 ft.**　Up the crack steeply to a good stance.

2　**70 ft.**　A shattered groove leads up the wall behind the stance to meet large overhangs. Move R. below these to a ramp leading into the corner, and turn the bulge in this (crux) by semi-layback technique to a good stance in the upper groove.

3　**70 ft.**　Go straight up the easier upper groove to the top.

104　Octo

HVS. 160 ft. ** *Brown, Sorrall, Belshaw, 1952.*
The R. hand section of the E. face of the Pinnacle has a great wall with obvious corner cracks up each side. The L. one which divides at half height gives the line of Gargoyle, HVS, a rather unbalanced

route; whilst the R. one gives Octo, a route of great beauty and interest.

Start at the foot of the corner which is reached by an exciting scramble up very steep grass from the Gully bed.

1   **50 ft.**   Climb the L. hand crack by semi-layback to reach a stance in the chimney above.

2   **110 ft.**   Climb up the chimney on its R. wall to an old peg in the overhang, and with protection from this, move out round the roof to get bridged in the crack above. (One can now look down and in at one's second!) The crack gives continually interesting climbing until it eases and an exit can be made on the R., and less strenuous climbing follows to a large grassy stance. Scrambling up R. leads to the top.

The Hand Traverse ES— (105), goes L. from the large grassy stance.

105   Pinnacle Arête and the Hand Traverse. (3)

ES— 270 ft. ** Boyson, Mortlock, 1962, Banner, Jones, 1960.

The combination of these two routes gives a route of a high degree of difficulty yet with plenty of protection. It is ideal for the technically proficient climber with a strong sense of survival. It starts just R. of the edge of the two faces of the Pinnacle, crosses this arête, and finishes up the steep walls above and to the L. of Octo.

Start below the first corner on the front face of the Pinnacle, directly above the finish of Llithrig.

1   **90 ft.**   Climb up the corner for 30 ft. (this is Taurus, ES—, which turns the roof above on the L. by some very hard climbing). Now move out L., steeply, but on large holds, to an old peg. Step L. again to the arête and up this with possibly a sling for aid, to better holds and a peg. A stance in slings can be taken here, using the peg and numerous nuts, etc. and so avoiding rope drag on the crux.

2   **30 ft.**   Crux. Traverse L. for 15 ft. on very small holds to reach a loose groove and climb this to a good stance and peg belay.

3   **30 ft.**   Straight on to reach another good ledge which leads L. to the top of Octo.

4   100 ft.   Move down L. to a foothold at the start of an exposed diagonal hand traverse. Stretch out and place a sling for aid, and then move into this. Now hand traverse across to a peg, and using this for aid, stand below a thin crack. Climb the thin crack with difficulty, but good protection to reach better holds and easier climbing up past an arch to a good stance.

5   20 ft.   Easily up the corner to the top.

106   Pinnacle Flake. (6)

*HVS+   180 ft. * Brown and Whillans, 1952.*
This route gives superb climbing in a tremendous situation. Protection is not good, and steadiness essential on the part of the leader. The most obvious feature of the wall on the R. of Taurus is a great flake on the R. and at half height. An HVS−, Spillikin, climbs the L. part of this wall, starting a few ft. R. of Taurus, whilst this route climbs the R. part, using the flake itself.

   Start on a shelf above and to the R. of the top of Pigott's Climb. It can be reached by one of the lower routes or by a traverse from the Eastern Terrace. (The Direct Finish to the East Buttress VS starts here also.) Peg belays essential.

1   50 ft.   Move out across the wall with difficulty to reach a ledge on the face. Go up the face from ledge to ledge until a very hard mantelshelf can be made, and higher ledges reached which lead across to the foot of the flake.

2   35 ft.   Climb the crack between the flake and the wall to a stance on the flake.

3   95 ft.   Move out delicately onto the arête on the R., and climb this on good holds to the top. A delightful pitch.

107 The Boulder. (7)

*HVS. 345 ft. ** Brown, 1951.*
The routes on the Pinnacle, and those on the R. half of the East Buttress, all finish on the great diagonal, scree-filled fault line known as the Eastern Terrace, which is joined also by the Green Gallery, the ledge which separates the East Buttress from the Pinnacle. *Eastern Terrace is the usual means of descent, in its lower section passing under a great face which marks the L. edge of the West Buttress, and then descending rock and steep grass above Middle Rock to join the path below the East*

Buttress just below the Corner. The first West Buttress route to be described ascends the great face above this terrace, and is reached via the lower scramble. It gives an exposed and quite delicate route, going diagonally across the face and finishing near the wet, great R. hand corner (Black Cleft, HVS+ **w**).

Start directly below the L. edge of the face, below an arête.

1   **150 ft.**   Climb straight up the arête to a peg belay. (Left Edge, HVS−, goes up this arête, a little to the L., with one peg runner). A traverse line can be seen to the R. and an old peg with a ring can be used for protecton. (Back rope for the second if required). Dubious undercut holds on a nose lead up R. to the traverse, and this is followed, with poor protection, to reach a sloping ledge. Balance across this to reach better holds leading up to a stance and belays about 15 ft. from Black Cleft.

2   **45 ft.**   Climb the thin crack on the L. until a nice move is possible through the overhang.

3   **150 ft.**   Scrambling and easy slabs L. then R. to the top.

108   Longland's Climb. (8)
VS. 340 ft. * *Longland, others, 1928.*
This is the first route on the West Buttress proper, climbing a line of slab just R. of Black Cleft. It gives very enjoyable climbing with two quite hard sections which contrast considerably.

Start by descending below the Boulder until a small gully and a traverse behind a huge flake lead to the foot of the slab.

1   **90 ft.**   Climb out onto the slab and up it, and sometimes the chimney beside it, to a stance where the chimney widens.

2   **40 ft.**   Up the chimney for a short distance, then out onto the slab and, from where it narrows, mantelshelf onto the wall on the R. Up this more easily to stances and belays.

3   **120 ft.**   Up the slab edge on good holds, well protected, to reach a large, crevassed ledge on the R.

4   **30 ft.**   The crux. Assemble on the R. hand edge of the large ledge, below an overhanging arête. The ascent of this is quite strenuous, and should be protected if possible. (It can be avoided by pitch 7 of White Slab round the corner on the R. More exposed but less strenuous.)

5 60 ft. Easily up a short chimney on the R.,
then broken rocks to the top.
This, and the three following routes, finish on the
flat top of the West Buttress. *The usual descent is via
the Eastern Terrace although. if rucksacks are carried up
the routes, it is a pleasant walk R. wards down the ridge,
and then along the valley floor back to the car park.*

109 White Slab. (9)

*HVS+ 560 ft. *** Moseley, Smith, 1956.*
One of the truly great slab routes of Britain, this
climb takes the West Buttress at its highest, following
a sustained, delicate line up the steep, light coloured
slab which narrows near its middle, and finishes a
little below the overhang of Longland's Climb. It is
the next complete slab line to Longland's.

Start by descending below Middle Rock to reach
the lowest part of the West Buttress. The first feature
is a very wet groove below Longland's, then a smooth,
red coloured section, then a smaller wet groove.
This route reaches the second groove by a traverse
just above the overhangs, about 15 ft. up. The climbing begins at a small, shattered pillar on the R. of
these.

1 60 ft. From the top of the pillar (runner), step
down and traverse delicately L. along the lip of the
overhangs. Go up a little on the R. of the wet groove
and then cross this to shattered rock and a good
stance and belays 15 ft. to the L. If one rope is left
through the first runner, the second can be protected
on the first, crucial section.

2 80 ft. Step back R. to reach a groove leading
through overhangs and a grassy crack line leading
finally to a ledge with fine spike belays, just R. of the
slab proper.

3 120 ft. Climb back down a little, and traverse
delicately out onto the slab using well worn holds
which come in from the L. (This is part of Sheaf in
reverse.) Go delicately up the edge of the slab with
a peg for protection (**Plate 30**) to a good spike after
60 ft. The next few ft. are very thin and usually a
peg is used to reach better holds leading back to the
arête at another spike. Now step round the corner
and traverse L. into a groove and go up this for
20 ft. to a stance and peg belays. (With an unsure
second it is better to stance on the arête on the R.,

Plate 30. On White Slab, pitch 3 at the first peg

using a long belay plus small, line ones. It also allows the leader to examine the next pitch!)

4 45 ft. From the footholds on the arête, lasso a small spike in the grooves on the far side of the slab (four casts seem usual) and then use the rope to swing across the slab and so up to the spike. Now climb more easily L. back onto the narrowing of the slab, and so to a small stance and peg belays.

5 120 ft. Go straight up the edge of the slab for 60 ft., all interesting, to reach the top of a rib. Climb up a little on the R. and then step back L. to a piton. From above the piton it is possible to traverse R. to an evil corner, and to get up this, but it is better to continue straight up the slab to its finish. Peg belay.

6 40 ft. Walk L. along grass, and then step down to join Longland's just before the crevassed stance. Up to this stance.

7 35 ft. Traverse below the overhang and step onto an exposed wall. Up this delicately R. to rejoin Longland's.

8 60 ft. Up a chimney and broken rock to the top.

110 The Sheaf. (10)

*HVS— 440 ft. ** Campbell, Cox, 1945.*
This very good route climbs the sheaf of ribs and corners just R. of White Slab. It reaches them by a traverse from the L.

    Start at the foot of Longland's.

1 35 ft. Descend R. to a small stance under the edge of the main slab.

2 50 ft. Make a hard move onto a ledge on the R., and from this step round onto the slab. This is the edge of White Slab, and a short traverse brings the first few ft. of its third pitch into reach. Down this part with difficulty, then up onto a good ledge and loose spike belays. (This is the crux of Narrow Slab, vs+, Linnell's Leap, a fine piece of climbing.)

3 85 ft. Descend for a few ft., then step round the corner onto the next layer of slabs. (Narrow goes round to the next slab.) Climb the slab to a ledge and continue up the slab above to reach a large stance in a corner.

4 70 ft. Go L. up the steep slab until holds lead round the corner into a small chimney (White joins here). Traverse across L. and up the slab to a peg stance as for White.

5 60 ft. Crux. Step R. from the stance to reach a

Plate 31. Great Slab – first pitch

difficult little groove. Go up this to below an overhang. Fix runners in the corner, and out on some spikes on the overhang, then swing out onto this and so mantel-shelf into an upper groove. Layback up this to a sitting stance in a corner.

6 60 ft. Ignore the groove above and make a wide stride out onto the R. hand rib. Pull round this boldly and so reach good holds and then easier, grassy climbing at the top of Narrow Slab.

7 80 ft. Easily up grass to join Longland's near top.

111 Great Slab. (11)

VS. 620 ft. *** **w** *Kirkus, MacPhee, 1930.*

An excellent route, mostly at s standard, giving interesting climbing. A serious undertaking, for unlike the harder routes, there are no easier ways up the buttress. The pitches described are long in order that the best stances may be used. Poor stances may be found to break these pitches, but their use is inadvisable. The great slab itself is high on the cliff and in fact, gives the easier part of the route.

Start well R. of White Slab where there is a weakness in the overhangs. About 150 ft. up the Western Terrace which runs up below this half of the buttress. A small rock tower shows the way.

1 130 ft. From the top of the small tower, move with difficulty onto an overhung slab leading L. A high runner may be fixed to give both leader and second protection before a delicate traverse L. is made (crux) to reach a long, narrow slab leading up L. Climb this slab, at first in the corner (**Plate 31**), and later on its edge, to reach a large stance and a cave. (Poor stance at 80 ft.)

2 150 ft. Step round onto the rib on the R. and climb it until it gets hard, then traverse R. to a good spike, and from this descend to reach a small overhang on the R. Bridge up this, and then climb rock and steep grass to reach a stance below the obvious corner. (Stance possible 15 ft. above the traverse R.)

3 60 ft. Climb the corner, going out onto the slab at half height for a few ft. Then back up the upper section to reach good runners. Next, move up the line of weakness in the slab on the L. to a good stance. (This pitch becomes the crux if it is wet.)

4 150 ft. Easier climbing diagonally across the slab. Good holds in a fine position. (Stance at 75 ft.)

5 130 ft. Climb up the arête on the L. to reach

easy ground and the top.

112 Slanting Slab. (12)
ES— 450 ft. ** *Whillans, Betts, 1955.*

This route, and Red Slab, start high on the Western
Terrace, and are reached by scrambling up the
lower part of this. It is a serious, hard climb in a
tremendous situation. Retreat could be very difficult
after the first pitch, and all members of the party
need to be very competent.

Start 60 ft. L. of Red Slab, where a pinnacle sticks
up below 10 ft. overhangs. Pegs usually visible
around the edge of the slab.

1 120 ft. Climb the pinnacle and then use 3 or 4
pegs to get out round the roof and onto the slab.
Climb L. on small holds to a welcome grass ledge,
then continue just below a bulge to a grass rake
leading up to a stance back on the R.

2 40 ft. (It is better if the second leads this easier
pitch). Climb the rake to its end then step round
the corner into a crack below a slab. Go up the
corner a little to a poor stance but excellent belays.

3 140 ft. Climb the flake to an overhang and then
traverse L. to reach a quartzy slab. Up this to another
bulge whence a step R. brings good holds for a swing
into an out-of-balance corner above. Leave this corner
after one move to climb the arête on its R., and
continue R. to better holds near a small niche and
exit R. to a good stance. Peg belays.

4 150 ft. Easy grass climbing to the top.

*Descend to the R. to reach the top of Western Terrace and
down this.*

113 Red Slab
HVS+ 300 ft. ** *Streetly, 1952.*

A very delicate slab climb giving an excellent problem without good protection. However the really
hard section is quite short.

Start high on the Western Terrace, at the bottom
R. hand side of a great, red slab which is overhung
on two sides and undercut. A large flake gives a way
through the lower roofs.

1 100 ft. From the flake, step L. to a flake below
the slab proper. Climb the corner to fix a good
runner and then step down and traverse out onto
the slab. A few moves L. and then a step back R.
gives access to a thin crack and this is used to pass a

slight bulge. Move L. to good holds (runners) and move up with difficulty to stand on these. Above, the slab is very steep, but to the L., it is just climbable on bulges and minute holds. Take this line (crux) moving towards the overhangs and then step round these to reach a small stance in a corner. Piton belays.

2   90 ft.   Climb the corner to fix a runner, then descend and from the stance, traverse very delicately L. to reach a faint rib. Up this and more traversing following a line of holds going gently up L. towards the end of the overhangs. Continually interesting climbing leads finally to grass and a good stance.

3   110 ft.   Easily up the gully behind to reach the top of the crag.

114   The Mostest

ES— 320 ft. *** Brown, 1957.

This fine route lies on the Far East Buttress and gives very hard climbing on an exposed and steep buttress. Protection is excellent throughout making it a good choice for the married hardman.

Start by descending the gully L. of the buttress until it peters out. Woubits, a climb of similar standard but poorly protected and on loose rock, climbs the wall a little before the end of the gully.

1   120 ft.   Step out from the end of the gully to reach the foot of a groove, and go up this to a steep little slab. Climb this by using cracks and continue up a short gully to reach a shattered pinnacle. Traverse L. to another groove and up this to a big grass stance and old peg belay. The unpleasant part of the route is now over (and the easy section!).

2   90 ft.   A crack leads up L. to the top of a pinnacle, from which holds go R. to a niche and a steep slab. Up this until a bold swing can be made round the corner onto the main wall. Climb this to a good runner. Now descend R., until a series of hard moves can be made up the steep wall above to reach a minute corner stance. Peg belays.

3   60 ft.   Climb the corner on good holds. It ends at a large roof with a fine peg. Move out L. to a foot-hold, and with protection (?) from a wood wedge or a nut, make a hard move L. to reach better holds and the end of the difficulties. Climb the groove above to a stance.

4   50 ft.   The delightfully easy slab to the top.

Crib Y Ddysgl. Cyrn Las

NE. Facing. 2,000 ft. above sea level. 600 ft. high.
G.R. 615559.

This steep cliff stands in Cwm Glas Mawr, high on
the R. hand side. It can be reached from near Ynys
Ettws by following the steep path up into the cwm,
and then leaving this path where an easy stream
crossing and traverse lead to the foot of scree cone
below the crag. ¾ hr. from the road to the start of
the routes.

Parking places as for the Three Cliffs, also rescue
facilities.

The crag itself is composed of three buttresses, all
of which start about 300 ft. above the screes, above
an area of heather slabs. The steep central buttress
contains both routes described and is known as the
Great Buttress. It is divided from the more grassy L.
buttress by a deep gully, Great Gully (VD+) which
gives a fine winter route, whilst the L. hand buttress
itself gives one poor route, Central Route (VD). To
the R. of the Great Buttress is a narrow, well marked
gully (Schoolmasters', s−) with broken, uninteresting rock on its R. The routes on the Great Buttress
are reached by scrambling diagonally in from either
side.

Generally, the climbing on this cliff is of a high
standard, rivalling the Cloggy routes for length,
exposure and beauty of technique. The two described
are the best on the cliff, each giving sustained climbing
at its standard on rock which is usually firm and
clean.

115   Main Wall

*S+ 465 ft. *** w Roberts, Cooke, 1935.*
One of the greatest of British severes, this route gives
magnificent climbing on the exposed L. edge of the
Great Buttress, finishing up the obvious slab near the
top. A serious expedition needing good climbing and
rope technique, and careful belaying.

Start about 300 ft. up the lower scramble, leaving
the path to scramble a further 50 ft. steeply to below
the L. hand side of the buttress. Well worn.

1   **70 ft.**   From a small ledge, a slabby series of
rakes goes up L. towards grass ledges. Quite steep.
From the end of these ledges, a small corner is
followed for 10 ft. and then a move R. onto an over-

Plate 32. Main Wall at the foot of the arête on pitch 4

hung slab from which spikes lead out R. to a pulpit stance.

2   80 ft.   A gangway slopes up R. towards a dark corner chimney. Follow this, and then the chimney until another ledge traverses out L. to reach a small stance on the edge of the buttress. Piton belay essential.

3   45 ft.   Good holds steeply R. lead to a large triangular ledge below a corner. (Subsidiary Groove, HVS+, takes a direct line up much of this section.)

4   90 ft.   Climb down a few ft. and make a stride across to a flake on the L. Go up to stand on this and then make an awkward pull up into a small niche. Escape from this by traversing L. onto the very edge of the buttress and so round to a ledge below the arête (**Plate 32**). Climb this steep arête on good, small holds and, after crossing a shallow groove, make a stance on a square ledge on the crest above the last stance.

5   80 ft.   Traverse L. across slabs to reach a chimney. Up this for 20 ft. until good holds can be followed L. across the base of a fine slab to overlook Great Gully. Climb this delightful edge with a final mantel-shelf move to a good stance at the top.

6   100 ft.   An odd little groove on the L. and then a slab lead to scrambling and the top of the crag.

To descend, either go well over into upper Cwm Glas, to reach the usual walking path down, or go well to the R. of the crag and down steep grass etc.

116   The Grooves

*HVS+ 370 ft. *** Brown, Cowan, Price, 1953.*
Just to the L. of Schoolmaster's Gully, on the Great Buttress, L.-ward slanting grooves lead up to near the final overhangs. This route follows these grooves, and gives sustained climbing, separated by large stances. The individual pitches are serious, but can be well protected, so giving a very enjoyable climb.

Start below the first groove. Best reached by walking in from the R.

1   120 ft.   After a few ft., an overhang gives a sharp problem, and provides access to a small ledge on the L. Now climb a slab to return to the corner and swing over a second bulge on excellent holds. For the remainder of the pitch, short, hard sections are divided by good resting places, always in a groove (feet can get greasy on this part). With a final steep move a good grassy stance is reached.

2   20 ft.   An easy little wall leading to a well worn stance below the second groove. (Escape is possible here via a traverse R. below overhangs. The crux of Green Caterpillar, VS!).

3   120 ft.   Get up a little rib and then make a very hard step into an open groove. Up this to reach an overhang, then turn and swing out L. to reach the groove proper. This gives 60 ft. of sustained hard climbing with finger and fist jamming being the most useful techniques, until a final little bulge leads to a small corner ledge. From this ledge, continue steeply up the corner for a few ft. until an exit can be made R. to another large ledge. (One can escape R. with a little abseil).

4   110 ft.   The usual finish is now described, but for those who have found the lower pitches fairly easy, a more difficult finish is possible, Overhanging Arête, ES — by first climbing a corner well to the R., then traversing out onto the arête above the stance and climbing this with a peg for aid. However, to finish in keeping both in standard and in line with the lower pitches, step up onto the sloping ledge above the stance and follow this L. round a corner to the bottom of a steep corner. Climb this using large, dubious holds until a hard move (sometimes with a peg) can be made out of the corner onto easier rock. which leads to the top.

Two other routes on this crag are worthy of mention, both steep lines up the crest of the Great Buttress giving climbing of increasing difficulty on very steep rock. They are the Great Buttress, ES — and the Skull, ES.

Crib Y Ddysgl. Clogwyn Y Person and Clogwyn Y Ddysgl

NW. Facing. About 2,500 ft. above sea-level. 200–400 ft. high. G.R. 616554

This pair of crags lies high on the mountain and form the end and the R. hand face of the ridge which runs down from Crib Y Ddysgl, and which divides the upper Cwm Glas into two smaller cwms. They can be reached either by following the path to Cyrn Las and continuing up into the higher cwm, or by a long traversing walk from Pen Y Pass around the N. ridge of Crib Goch above Dinas Mot. However,

Plate 33. On the Parson's Nose

the best method is to do a route on Cyrn Las and then to walk easily across the cwm to the cliffs. Time for walking from Ynys Ettws is about an hr., or from Pen Y Pass, an hr. and a half.

Rescue facilities and parking as for the Three Cliffs. Also parking at Pen Y Pass for that approach.

The name Clogwyn Y Person refers only to the end section of the cliff, which is divided from the main crag by a cleft and has the form of a nose. Clogwyn Y Ddysgl is a long crag whose base and top rise together as the ridge approaches the summit of the mountain. The only really obvious feature is a crack above a huge fallen block about 150 yds. R. of the cleft.

Climbing generally is in the lower grades with some fine mountaineering routes. The rock is very good on the L. section of the cliff, but deteriorates to the R.

117   The Parson's Nose Route

*D+ 250 ft. * w Stocker, 1884.*
The nose is climbable in many places, both up the face and up each supporting gully, *Western Gully (M) being the easiest and therefore the usual descent.* This route is the classic line up the nose and gives fine exposed climbing on good holds.

Start at the lowest point of the nose below slabs.
1   **80 ft.**   Up the slabs.
2   **70 ft.**   Up steeper slabs trending slightly towards Western Gully (**Plate 33**) to a stance in a faint line of weakness.
3   **50 ft.**   Traverse R. along a thin crack to reach the edge of the Gully.
4   **50 ft.**   Easily up the edge to the top.

118   Gambit Climb

*VD+ 320 ft. * Thompson, Jones, Orton, 1910.*
This classic route lies nearly halfway between Western Gully and the fallen block. It climbs the steep lower wall via cracks and a slab, and then above up various interesting cracks and chimneys.

Start at a flake crack leading up to a L. ward sloping slab.
1   **60 ft.**   Climb the crack until a step L. leads to the slab with runners. Across this to reach a steep crack which finishes at a good ledge and belays.
2   **15 ft.**   Jam up the crack to reach a large stance.

3 50 ft. Traverse R. to reach a chimney. Up this to a grass ledge.

4 45 ft. Traverse R. with difficulty to a short chimney and climb this to another good ledge.

5 70 ft. Climb the chimney at the back to the top of a pinnacle, and then hand-traverse into the easy corner crack and so reach a scree-covered ledge.

6 80 ft. Walk R. up grass to a steep corner with a finger crack which leads strenuously to the top.

Scrambling leads to the ridge above, the Clogwyn Y Person Arête which gives a grade E climb, either up to the summit, or *down to the top of Western Gully (M) and so down via this*.

119 The Ring

*VS— 350 ft. * Harding, Disley, 1948.*
This steep and interesting route lies mid-way between Gambit and the fallen block.

Start up a steep corner R. of two chimneys.

1 50 ft. Start up the groove, but as this is very hard, step out L. round a corner and go up for 20 ft. to some piled blocks and so above these to a good stance.

2 40 ft. Move up then traverse L. to a corner to reach a series of rocky steps which lead to another stance.

3 50 ft. Climb the corner for 15 ft. then step L. and continue up the wall above on small holds. Mantel-shelf onto a small stance and traverse R. to reach another with a better belay.

4 50 ft. Traverse awkwardly L. across a small slab then climb up to a short chimney. Continue up the crack to a stance by a perched block.

5 70 ft. Traverse L. and go up a cracked corner, runners, then continue up a wall to reach a slab below a steep corner.

6 90 ft. Climb the corner first by the L. hand crack to a good ledge, then step R. and climb twin cracks strenuously to the top.

120 Fallen Block Crack

*VS. 265 ft. ** Waller, 1927.*
A really great route, usually climbed in boots! Start above the fallen block.

1 30 ft. Up the initial crack strenuously to a chockstone belay.

2 85 ft. Crux. Get round the overhang and up

the steep crack above to a very welcome resting place. Either climb the chimney or the thin crack on its R., and finally take the easier chimney above to a large stance.

3 30 ft. Climb a chimney on the L.

4 120 ft. Continue easily in the same line to the top of the crag.

121   Rectory Chimneys

*VD. 270 ft. * **w** Guinness, 1925.*

A very good route of its standard, finding a steep way up the walls to the R. of Fallen Block Crack.

Start about 80 ft. R. of Fallen Block Crack at a chimney with a leaning flake.

1 60 ft. Climb the chimney and then the groove above.

2 35 ft. Up a short wall to reach an obvious crack. Up this.

3 35 ft. Avoid the continuation of the crack by a traverse L. to enter the other side of the crack. Stance after 15 ft.

4 40 ft. After one move in the corner, follow a delightful traverse to reach a large chimney. Climb this to a good ledge.

5 100 ft. Straight ahead with less difficulty.

122   The Rosy Crucifixion

*HVS+ 200 ft. * Crew and Ingle, 1963.*

Well to the R., and much higher than the rest of the crag, is a large triangular buttress of slabs. A VS+, The Infidel, follows the R. hand edge of these, whilst this route takes the wall to its L.

Start 150 ft. up the lower slabs at the foot of an obvious red flakey crack (The Infidel).

1 120 ft. Climb first diagonally L. to a tiny ledge level with the foot of the crack. Continue L. up to a blind flake crack and climb this with difficulty to a small, loose spike. Traverse R. to a good ledge in the middle of the wall. Move up 10 ft. then take a thin, slanting crack (peg) which leads to the foot of a bottomless groove on the R. Climb this groove (peg) to a small roof, and step L. to a long, narrow ledge. Belays on the L.

2 80 ft. Follow a steep line of cracks on the R. on good holds, moving L. near the top. Continue more easily to ledge and belays near the edge (junction with the Infidel).

The gully at the head of this cwm is called Parsley Fern Gully and gives an excellent winter route, often with a corniced exit.

Llanberis Pass. South Side. Dinas Mot
N. Facing. 1,000 ft. above sea level. 600 ft. high.
G.R. 626563. Plate 34.

The collection of cliffs known as Dinas Mot lies a few hundred ft. above the Llanberis Pass road, opposite Dinas Cromlech. It can be reached by walking from Pont Y Cromlech or from Ynys Ettws in under 20 mins.

Parking and rescue facilities as for Dinas Cromlech.

This fine crag gives widely differing types of climbing, both on its buttresses and even on the routes themselves. The old climbing ground of the Nose is the obvious smooth, triangular central area of slab which is divided from the other buttress by gullies which provide obvious descents. *The* L. *hand Eastern Gully,* D —, *is rather unpleasant, but Western Gully,* D —, *is excellent.* Above and L. of the Nose is the Eastern Wing which gives very steep, hard climbing, whilst to the R. stretches the long Western Wing, cut by gullies on the R., which provides hard routes of great variety, but unfortunately, often marred by grass traverses in their upper section. Climbing on the Nose is quite delicate on delightfully firm rock whilst the Wings give mostly hard, steep routes, very much in the modern idiom.

123 The Cracks
S+ (VS— on pitch 6) 260 ft. * *Bathurst, Bathurst, 1930.*
Four routes are described on the Nose, one up each edge, one up the central, light-coloured groove, and a hard route which climbs across the smooth central section. This route takes the L. edge and is the easiest route on the buttress.

Start on the L. of the lowest rocks of the base of the Nose.

1 40 ft. Easy climbing leads up R. to a shallow groove which ends at a small stance on the R.

2 50 ft. Step L. onto a sloping slab and follow this, generally moving L., to reach a short groove with a crack and so to a stance with holly trees.

3 30 ft. Make a delicate traverse R. using undercut holds to a well worn chimney. Up this to a stance

Plate 34. Dinas Mot

SLC

B S   DD

on a sharp flake.

4 50 ft.   Move L. to a dirt ledge and climb twin cracks until the R. hand one ends, and an exposed move is made up L. to easy ground and a large terrace on the edge of Eastern Gully.

5 45 ft.   Walk across to a large pinnacle and from it, step R. to reach another ledge below cracks. Follow the L. crack to another stance near the edge.

6 45 ft.   Crux. Climb up a line of ledges leading R. to a narrow shelf. Now after fixing a running belay, mantel-shelf onto the next ledge, rounded and exposed. Finally, easily to the top. This pitch can be avoided, either by stepping L. into the gully, or by climbing the arête above the stance (s).

124   The Direct Route

VS. 245 ft. *** Kirkus, Cooper, MacPhee, 1936.
This is one of the great vs's of Wales, climbing delicately up the central faint depression of the Nose, and then finishing up the steep crack above.

Start at the lowest part of the Nose.

1 50 ft.   Scramble up easy rock to reach a pedestal then step up L. to reach the first stance of the Cracks.

2 90 ft.   Climb up R. until a traverse and a mantel-shelf move brings one to the bottom of the groove. Now go L. up a ramp until small holds lead back into the corner. Awkward moves round a slight steepening lead to a shallow scoop with a high, small spike runner. Above this, after a few more good moves, the angle relents and an open area of stance is reached.

3 50 ft.   Climb up R., easily, to a small pulpit, from which a well worn foothold leads out onto the very bridge of the nose. A long, low reach, or a hard hand-traverse (**Plate 35**) brings good holds into reach and a short ascent ends on a good flat ledge with huge flake belays.

4 55 ft.   The corner on the L. is extremely hard to start (shoulder?) but soon good holds are reached and followed by 'monkey up a stick' technique to gain a small stance. Above, an easier groove leads up L. to the top.

125   Diagonal Route

HVS− 240 ft. ** Birtwistle, Parkinson, 1938.
As it name implies, this fine route goes across the Nose, giving unusually open and unprotected climb-

Plate 35. Pitch 3 of The Nose Direct by the hand traverse

Plate 36. *Just reaching the pocket on pitch 3 of Diagonal Route*

ing. It finishes up the very steep corner at the top R. hand side.

Start as for Direct Route.

1 60 ft. Up a little as for Direct, then move across to reach a groove beside a detached flake. From the flake, traverse across R. until a very delicate move brings a small stance, below a small overhang, into reach. Peg belay or small spikes.

2 40 ft. Above is a large overhang. Go up towards this until good holds lead L. to a little ledge. A nut, or chockstone runner can be arranged in a slot here, and then the leader can either traverse very delicately across under the roof (very thin), or step back down and traverse low to reach good flake holds below and to the R. of the overhang (devious but safe). Either method leads thankfully to a V chimney which is followed to reach a fine stance and peg belay.

3 40 ft. Delicate toe traversing R. gives access to a steep groove. Once started, retreat seems impossible and so it is better to follow the awkwardly spaced holds to reach a rounded foot-hold on the R., on which it is possible to rest. For the next 8 ft., progress depends on a pocket on the R. (**Plate 36**) (nut runner in it, too) and then a delightfully easy crack is reached with stances and belays.

4 60 ft. Continue without difficulty up the crack and over ledges to a stance below the final corner.

5 40 ft. The crack is hard to start but a good resting ledge soon arrives. Above this, bridging on the L., leads up to a spike on the R. and an acrobatic few moments end, one hopes, in good holds being reached and hence the stance at the top.

126   Western Slabs

*VS. 200 ft. * Edwards, Edge, D'Aeth, 1931.*

The R. hand side of the Nose is composed of a smooth area of slabs above a short, vertical wall. This delightful route takes the easiest line up these slabs, keeping between the gully and a faint rib line which ends at the final corner of Diagonal Route. This rib gives the line of Western Rib (HVS−).

Start by the stone wall.

1 50 ft. First climb up onto a ledge, then go up on the L. until it is possible to traverse R. over a perched block and onto a long, grass ledge.

2 90 ft. Initially, the slabs are deceptively easy, but soon, after 20 ft., smaller holds lead L., up, and

Plate 37. Leader on Mole, pitch 2, just below the good runner. Other pair are on the last pitch of Gollum

then back R. to gain a long shallow groove, which ends at a stance on the edge of the Nose.

3   60 ft.   Back L. a few ft. and then easily up to another ledge. Now take a crack up a groove on the L. until a hard move out R. is possible onto the arête and this is followed to the top.

Descent from all the Nose routes is usually made by one of the gullies, but it is possible to continue above the Nose towards Crib Goch by going R. on quartz and then up a chimney and a corner. After a traverse L. scramble over blocks, past a cave to grassy slopes and walking country.

127   The Mole

HVS— 275 ft. ** Brown, Langmuir, 1961.

The Eastern Wing is a very steep tower above and to the L. of the Nose. A diagonal grass rake cuts across it at half height to give a vertical lower section and an upper half made up of very steep slabs and square cut roofs. This route gives a fine introduction to the style of climbing. It comes from high in the gully on the L. up the very steep slabs and walls on excellent rock.

Start at a small grass rake a little above the main one.

1   90 ft.   Up the grass to a steep slab. Climb this to a large grassy stance below a huge flake and large overhangs. (Gollum uses this stance also).

2   110 ft.   Climb up onto the flake and so reach a short arête (crux). Above this continue steeply R. to reach a diagonal slab. Climb the corner for 10 ft. to a good runner (**Plate 37**), then traverse R. and go up to another corner. Move down and R. with difficulty and then up L. past the overhangs to a stance and belays.

3   75 ft.   Up into the groove on the L., then back R. and up steeply on loose rock and grass to the top.

128   Gollum

HVS. 350 ft. * Webb, Harris, Cowley, 1964.

The Mole is the only really fine route up the L. side of the buttress, but the R. section has two excellent routes. Beorn (E s—) takes a line up near the arête of the crag across three impressive overhangs, whilst this route finds a good approach to the first grass rake and then goes through the overhangs to the R. of Mole's first stance. Good situations and very interesting climbing compensate for the lack of line.

Start at the top of a grass ridge at the lowest point of the crag.

1 40 ft. Follow a line of holds steeply R. to a peg from which a slab can be reached with a small stance above it.

2 60 ft. Move across into the groove and climb this on good holds to grass and finally a tree on the grass break. A fine pitch.

3 50 ft. Walk L. up grass to reach the first stance of Mole.

4 110 ft. Traverse R. across a slab to reach a good foothold below a slight break in the overhangs. Turn the overhangs with aid from a peg (crux) to reach a poor resting place below a short groove. (Beware of rope drag.) Delicately up the groove and then boldly up L. to reach better holds, and after a few ft., the second stance of Mole.

5 90 ft. Traverse R. below small roofs (**Plate 37**) to reach a steep arête. Up this in excellent position.

129 Black Spring

*HVS. 540 ft. ** Boyson, Williams, 1965.*
The Western Wing is a very large area of rock broken by two gullies into three distinct areas. *The L. of these gullies, Jammed Boulder Gully (M) provides a suitable way down in dry weather*, whilst the R. one, deep and dark looking, is Black Cleft, the third of the routes described in this area. Between Western Gully and Jammed Boulder Gully is a large area of rock divided by a grass terrace, giving numerous routes and variations, all interchangeable. This superb hard route takes a central line up the water-streaked L. hand slab. To its L., another very good route, Black Shadow, (HVS) goes near the arête of Western Gully.

Start a few ft. R. of Western Gully.

1 50 ft. Straight up the wall via a crack to a grass ledge. (Peg belay).

2 90 ft. A crack goes up the wet slabs above. Climb this until it gets hard, then traverse L., surprisingly in better balance than in the crack, until pockets lead up deviously to a rib and so to a little cave stance. Peg belay. A continually surprising pitch.

3 110 ft. Go over the roof above the stance to reach a steep slab. Go up this moving L. when in doubt to reach a prominent quartz crack in easier ground. Up the crack to the grass break.

4   120 ft.   Fairly easy climbing up broken rocks and grass above past two little trees to reach a steep wall below a large roof.

5   120 ft.   Laybacking up the crack to below the roof is followed by a long, easy traverse R. to reach a stance where the roof ends.

6   50 ft.   Easy slabs to the top (*or descend grass and slabs diagonally to the R. to regain easy ground at the foot of the crag*).

130   Slow Ledge Climb by Dolerite Dump Start

S+ 445 ft. * Edwards, Gask, 1934.

The lower part of this climb takes the central area to the grass break whilst the top section gives good, continuous climbing in a fine situation. The famous Slow Ledge, 'a position of romantic exposure' is a sloping shelf just above a large overhang.

Start 20 yds. R. of Western Gully, to the L. of some quartz.

1   120 ft.   Climb easily up to the bottom of an overhanging crack, traverse L. and up rounded rocks to a stance below another crack, which is climbed to reach easier rocks and a grass ledge below a steep wall. Walk L. to a good belay below a prominent deep L facing corner.

2   50 ft.   Climb the corner, usually greasy, to a belay well back.

3   100 ft.   Climb a steep loose corner above to a good ledge. Difficult. Now go L. up grass to a stance on the large grass break.

4   50 ft.   The Slow Ledge is now directly above. Walk L. and from a corner get out onto a rib. Up this with perched blocks to a line of steps and a crevasse below an overhang at 30 ft. Traverse R. across a slab, and finally, semi hand traverse to reach the Slow Ledge itself. The reason for its name should now be apparent.

6   25 ft.   Step R. and go up until another hand traverse and a mantel-shelf leads R. to a grassy bay.

7   100 ft.   Go straight up for 15 ft. then step L. across a rib and climb this, zigzagging to avoid difficulties, and finally scrambling to the top of the crag.

131   Black Cleft

VD+ 390 ft. **w** *Thompson, 1897.*

A classic gully climb, one of the few really good ones

in the Pass, taking the R. hand of the two gullies which cut the cliff on the R.

Start at the foot of the gully.

1 80 ft. Scramble up the introductory section.

2 40 ft. A narrow section with a chockstone turned on the L.

3 60 ft. The bed is now water worn and steep, giving the crux pitch.

4 60 ft. Follow the gully with continual interest.

5 150 ft. Easier climbing up the less steep final section.

132 Plexus

*HVS. 450 ft. * Ingle and Crew, 1962.*

The R. section of this cliff is made up of steep slabs, partly vegetated, leading up to large overhangs with very steep climbing above. Three routes, Sexus (HVS+), Plexus, and Nexus (ES−) climb this buttress up the L. side, centre and R. side respectively, each giving a thin lower pitch followed by a short artificial section and then a very exposed final section. Plexus is rapidly losing any vegetation and loose rock to become a really great climb.

Start well to the R. of the cliff below a tree.

1 60 ft. Unpleasant climbing up heather to the tree and then traverse L. to reach a small stance below a shallow groove.

2 150 ft. Get onto the little grass ledge below the groove. Use a peg to pass an initial bulge and step R. to a small slab. Climb up L. to a crack and up this, at first R., then back L. on good holds to an arête and slab climbing to a stance below the over-hangs. Peg belay.

3 120 ft. A few ft. R., the overhang is split by a groove. Use a peg to get into this and then step L. into a faint groove. Climb this and a very thin slab on the R. to reach a jammed block and a relenting of the difficulty. Go over the block and use a L.-wards leading ledge to reach a short slab. Continue L. to reach a good stance.

4 120 ft. Grooves and slabs lead fairly easily to the top.

Besides the hard routes on this buttress, it is worth noting a VS−, Gardd (150 ft.) which gives a delight-ful pitch up the slab a little to the R. of the buttress. A bulge at the bottom provides the crux whilst a forked lightening crack gives the key to the final section. *Descent usually by abseil.*

Lliwedd
N. Facing. 2,350 ft. above sea level. 900 ft. high.
G.R. 623534.

This is the largest single crag in this guide book and
yet, due to its fairly easy angle and numerous breaks
and grassy ledges, it gives few really excellent routes.
It is, however, criss-crossed with over eighty routes
and variations. It lies on the L. hand loop of the
Snowdon Horseshoe above Llyn Llydaw and can be
reached easily from Pen Y Pass (GR 647556) by
following the Miners' Track to the lake and then
taking a diagonal path to the screes below the cliff.
1 hr. is normally sufficient to the foot of any route.

Parking at Pen Y Pass. Mountain rescue facilities
at Pen Y Gwryd Hotel (GR 660557).

The crag is made up of four buttresses divided by
three gullies. Central Gully (138) is the central fault
separating the main East and West Buttresses whilst
on the L. East Gully outlines the fault between East
Buttress and Far East Buttress and on the R. the
shallow Slanting Gully performs a similar task
between West Buttress and Slanting Buttress. The
best climbing lies on the East Buttress, mostly on its
lower half and five of the selected routes lie on this
section. Central Gully Direct, already mentioned,
gives the sixth route (and the hardest on the cliff,
HVS) whilst Slanting Buttress Ridge makes the best
of the rock on Slanting Buttress.

The East Buttress presents three facets. An open L.
side up which Horned Crag finds a fairly easy line.
A frontal face marked by two large grass ledges in
the lower reaches, the L. hand, higher one being the
very important Heather Shelf and the R. hand,
Birch Tree Terrace. Higher, perhaps two-thirds of
the way up the buttress is the Great Terrace which
drops R.-wards from the crest of this section. Finally a
R. section, separated from the others by a faint gully,
Shallow Gully, which slightly notches the skyline.
This section has a ledge at one-third height called
the Bowling Green.

133   Horned Crag Route
*D. 800 ft. * **w** Thomson, Eckenstein, 1905.*
This pleasant route, involving some interesting

climbing and some scrambling, goes up the L. half
of the East Buttress passing the prominent pinnacle
at half height.

Start as for the next two routes, on the Heather
Shelf which is reached by an M from below and to
the L. A good warming up pitch. Start at the L. hand
end.

1 60 ft.   Step down a few ft. and then traverse L.
across one faint rib to reach and climb a second,
easier rib. Move up L. over this into a faint groove
and reach a stance on the L. of this.

2 80 ft.   Go up L. onto yet another rib and follow
this pleasantly to a heather stance.

3 90 ft.   Follow the R. edge of the broader rib
above until it reaches another heather stance.

4 100 ft.   It is possible to continue direct (VD +)
but instead, go R-wards up the wall on a weakness
which includes a shallow chimney to a ledge well to
the R.

5 80 ft.   Scramble up L. to below the grey wall of
the Horned Crag.

6 30 ft.   Take the central groove easily to a stance
below a steeper groove.

7 40 ft.   Crux. Start in the groove but soon go out R.
and so follow the edge on good holds to a good stance.

8 20 ft.   Up L. between the horns.

9 100 ft.   Easily straight above up a wall, across
quartz and finally onto a rib.

200 ft. of scrambling remains to the summit where
walkers wait to be surprised.

134 Paradise/Terminal Arête

*VD + /M. 885 ft. * Jones, Blackwell, 1909.*
Three routes climb the wall above the Heather
Shelf; on the L., Yellow Slab (s) goes up to join
Horned Crag, whilst on the R. Purgatory (VS +)
climbs a groove which cuts the bulging wall above,
crossing Paradise at its first stance and again at its
third. Paradise takes the groove in the centre of the
wall.

Start below the groove which forks at 50 ft.

1 90 ft.   Climb the groove for 50 ft. and then take
the R. hand fork to a wall on the R. and so to a grass
ledge.

2 25 ft.   Purgatory takes the continuation of the
groove so instead, cross the ledge and go up to a
stance on the R.

3 80 ft. Climb a slabby groove on the L., with a difficult finish, to a slab, and continue easily to a good ledge.

4 90 ft. Climb the long groove on the L. of the rib above to easy ground. (Purgatory takes the rib direct.)

From here it is possible to return to the foot of this route by traversing 80 ft. L. and then climbing down Horned Crag. However, mountaineers will now follow a line of ribs up R. for 200 ft. easily, to reach a quartz boss on the crest of the Buttress. This marks the start of Terminal Arête, and lies at the upper end of the Great Terrace. (Hence Red Wall could be joined by a short (120 ft.) descending traverse on this terrace.) Terminal Arête (400 ft.) can be followed in about four pitches and scrambles to the summit of East Peak.

135 Avalanche/Red Wall

VD+ 870 ft. *** **w** *Thomson, Reynolds, 1907.*
This good climb traverses out R. from the Heather Shelf to take a steep line up the crest of the buttress to the Great Terrace and continues by picking out the best steep bits up the walls above. A good introduction to the crag.

Start at the R. end of the Heather Shelf which can be reached from directly below by an extra pitch if required.

1 100 ft. Make a long ascending traverse R. on fine holds until a rib leads up to a small stance below a grooved corner.

2 40 ft. Up the grooves on good holds until a ledge leads back R. to below a steeper section – The Quartz Sickle.

3 40 ft. Move awkwardly up R., then the bulges above force one L. to bridge into a steep crack and so to a small stance.

4 80 ft. Climb up onto the rib on the R. and follow this pleasantly to easier ground.

5 100 ft. Straight up easily to a grassy groove leading to a belay below a very steep wall.

6 100 ft. Walk R. up below the wall to reach the Great Terrace. Poor belays below a reddish wall with a noticeable jammed block. Slab lead up to its L., steep ribs to its R.

7 80 ft. Climb the slab until it steepens, level with the jammed block. Now move up delicately R. until small holds lead to a rib with an awkward last move onto a good stance.

8 100 ft. Continue up the rib above with a slightly harder move at the top. The ledge reached is the Gallery and marks the start of the final section of the climb – Longland's Continuation. There is a gully (Shallow Gully) on the R. Start 60 ft. in from this at a quartz outcrop below a rib.

9 80 ft. Climb the rib to a nook and then bridge up and step out R. onto slabs. Keep moving R. to arrive at a stance on a grassy gangway leading up L.

10 40 ft. Ignore the gangway and move R. again to follow another rib over blocks to a stance.

11 70 ft. Easily up the shattered rib above to a large stance, below a steep slab.

12 40 ft. Get onto the slab and climb it moving L., then over rocks to the summit.

136 The Sword/Route II

*S+/VD. 415 ft. * Edwards/Thompson, 1938/1904.*
Between Birch Tree Terrace and Shallow Gully, a fine grey buttress goes up the lower 200 ft. of the cliff. Route II starts up Shallow Gully but gets out onto the buttress about 150 ft. up at a break with a quartz boss on it – the Quartz Babe. The combination described takes the lower section direct to the Babe and then continues much more easily to the top.

A climber may prefer to descend Route II after climbing only The Sword.
Start a few ft. R. of the crest of the buttress near the bottom of Shallow Gully and about 40 yds. L. of Central Gully.

1 130 ft. A ledge on the crest is reached by a complicated series of moves diagonally up the R. wall of the ridge under some overhangs (crux). Next climb the rib direct by exciting (?) climbing which luckily gets easier. The rock is good and a rest may be found after 80 ft. However, it is best to continue to the Quartz Babe.

2 70 ft. Continue direct, very much easier, to a stance below a steep little wall.

3 25 ft. Climb direct up the R. side of the slab using the original 'Thank God' holds. Stance higher on the L.

4 50 ft. Go L. for 15 ft. to reach a groove. Climb this on good holds.

5 80 ft. Follow the groove more easily to a stance.

6   60 ft.   Easy rocks to the Great Terrace.

Continue as for Red Wall and Longland's continuation.

137   Bowling Green Buttress/Great Chimney

VS/VD+ 870 ft. * Mallory/Thomson, 1919/1907.
This combination selects the best and most difficult approach to the Bowling Green and a fine continuation to the top of the crag. The two sections gain by the contrasts of style and standard.

Three routes reach the Bowling Green up the ribs and slabs below it, Mallory's Slab (VD+) and Bowling Green Slab (S+) up the slightly gentler slabs on the L. and this route up the crest of the buttress nearest to the Central Gully depression.

Start below the buttress about 50 ft. below and to the L. of the quartz ledges in Central Gully.

1   90 ft.   Excellent climbing on small incut holds up the crest of the buttress.

2   80 ft.   Take the shallow groove above with increasing difficulty until a hard final move R. leads to easy ground.

3   60 ft.   Follow the edge on the L. to the Bowling Green.

It is possible to descend from here to the foot of the route by traversing R. to join the way off Central Gully Direct (138) or by traversing L. across Shallow Gully and various ribs 70 or 80 ft. to reach Route II, so down to the Quartz Babe from which a final descent of Route II can be made.

4   100 ft.   The chimney lies above the R. end of the Bowling Green above an ash tree on quartz ledges. It starts 40 ft. above the tree but is reached by a long (70 ft.) traverse from the L. so first climb up an easy groove until good holds at 30 ft. lead R. to reach the traverse line and so get to the Sentry Box at the foot of the chimney. If this approach is unfindable, then one must climb the other groove nearer the chimney with more difficulty.

5   100 ft.   Climb the chimney energetically, mainly on the L. wall.

6   80 ft.   Continue in the chimney, easier.

7   60 ft.   A final pitch leads to easy ground.

8   300 ft.   Scramble to the top of the crag.

138   Central Gully Direct

HVS. 160 ft. * Dodd and Edwards, 1938.
This intimidating route takes a direct line up the

back R. side of the lower bowl of the Central Gully. Steep climbing on loose, sometimes wet, greasy rock make it a must for the discerning 'hard' man. Nevertheless a fine climb.

Start directly below the corner crack about 150 ft. above the initial slabs at a quartz ledge. The second would be well advised to stand a little to one side (and to wear a crash helmet).

1 50 ft. Bridge up the steep curving corner until a thin layback move on the L. provides the key to the first overhang. Stance 10 ft. higher with thread belays.

2 110 ft. Continue up the crack for 75 ft. to a niche below a roof. Now climb this on the R. with difficulty to reach the easier angled part of the gully and stances in about 30 ft.

The rest of the gully to the top of the mountain is easy but if(!) P.A.'s are worn it is better to continue up for only about 40 ft. until a walking traverse can be made 60 ft. R. to a pinnacle out on West Peak. Now descend steeply but easily on large heather ledges until a little groove (D −) leads onto a line of ledges which lead back L. (facing in) to the foot of the climb.

139 Slanting Buttress Ridge Route

*D. 740 ft. * Abraham Bros., 1904.*

This route takes the easiest line up the crest of the large ill-defined buttress on the R. of Slanting Gully which itself gives a long scramble with a good hard (s +) slab pitch at half height and makes a great winter climb. A good bad weather route on large holds with adequate possibilities for protection.

Start at the foot of the ridge near some quartz outcrops below a gentle glacis.

1 100 ft. Up the centre of the glacis.

2 90 ft. Continue in the same line without difficulty.

3 120 ft. Another simple pitch up the gentle slabs to a stance on quartz below steeper wall.

4 75 ft. Up L. to two grooves. Climb the L. hand one by its L. wall, to a large ledge and continue to another quartz ledge below a steep nose.

5 35 ft. Up to the L. to follow a gangway to where the angle of the buttress eases.

6 120 ft. Continue by a chimney and then an arête to reach the main wall above.

7 60 ft. Traverse out R. and then by a narrow

ledge continue round a spur to reach grass ledges.
8   40 ft.   The crux. Continue by a central crack
to good ledge.
9   100 ft.   Easily L. then R. to the summit.

Llanberis Area. Outlying Climbs

140   The Wall. Craig Rhaeadr
*HVS. 360 ft. * Brown, Cain, Jones, 1959.*
N. Facing. 1,500 ft. above sea level. 350 ft. high.
G.R. 621561.
Although part of this crag is usually immersed in a
waterfall, nevertheless it adds another dimension to
the styles of climbing found in Llanberis Pass, and
so definitely it is worth a visit. It can be reached by
following the path up towards Cwm Glas from near
Ynys Ettws for about 25 mins.

Parking and mountain rescue facilities as for the
Three Cliffs.

The main features of the crag are an unpleasant
gully to the R. of the central waterfall, a large pinnacle,
the Pedestal, just L. of the waterfall, and finally, a large
detached pillar, Cwm Glas Pinnacle, well on the L.
An unpleasant 'classic' type route goes via the R. side
of the Pedestal and, after a shower bath traverse of
the sloping ledge above, finishes just L. of the gully,
Waterfall Climb (s+) **w**. Another wet route,
Chequered Wall (HVS−), climbs the L. side of the
Pedestal and then the walls above, turning the overhangs above on the L. However, the walls to the L.
of this route are usually drier, and give fine climbing,
marred by only a little grass. Red Wall (HVS−)
goes directly up the crag on red rock and grass above
the terrace mid-way between the Pinnacle and the
Pedestal. The Wall, the best route on this crag, goes
up the section of white rock on the L. of Red Wall.
Exciting, steep climbing with real difficulty only at
the crux. It is not affected by the waterfall and is
on good rock.

Start halfway between the Pinnacle and the Red
Wall.
1   140 ft.   Follow a traverse up steeply R. and then
move back L. to below a smooth, grooved wall. Go
up this for 20 ft. (crux) then R. on better holds for
50 ft. towards the L. edge of some grass ledges.
(Belays if required). Now go diagonally L. to a small,
grassy stance and peg directly above the crux.

2 150 ft.   Move L. for 10 ft., then go straight up on good holds to a V chimney which is followed to grass and easier rock. Up this direct for 40 ft. to a good grass ledge and a fine spike belay.

3 60 ft.   Climb the corner above, then easier climbing leads to the top of the crag.

141   Flake Chimney. Dinas Bach

D+ 100 ft. Carr, 1928 or before.
NE. Facing crag. 1,050 ft. above sea-level. 150 ft. high.
G.R. 631560.

This is a pleasant little crag lying on the Crib Goch side of the Llanberis Pass road between Pen Y Pass and Pont Y Gromlech. It can be reached direct from the road in about 10 mins. A little parking possible in laybys. Otherwise at Pen Y Pass.

Mountain rescue facilities as for Dinas Cromlech

The crag is in two sections separated by a tree-filled gully, Ash Tree Gully (D−). On the R. hand w. section two routes criss-cross. Wall and Traverse Climb (D+) traverses below overhangs until a groove leads up to the top, while Crack and Slab Climb (VD) starts 5 yds. L. of the wall and leads via a hard crack to the grass ledge and then continues up the walls above. However, the route selected is on the E. cliff up the R. side of the obvious flake and the wall above, while a fine little D+, Flake Traverse, takes the wall of Ash Tree Gully up flakes near the top, with harder routes taking the cracks in the slabs between these routes.

Start at the foot of the chimney.

1 50 ft.   Climb the chimney either deeply in or on the front edge.

2 50 ft.   Step across onto the wall and move R. to a good ledge and then continue by a crack to the top.

Up Flake Traverse and down Flake Chimney makes a good combination.

142   Reade's Route II. Crib Goch

*VD+ 220 ft. * Reade, Bartman, 1908.*
NW. Facing crag. 2,700 ft. above sea level. 250 ft. high
G.R. 623552.

This crag is situated directly below the pinnacle end of the Crib Goch ridge looking down into the Llanberis Pass. It can be reached from Cwm Glas or by traversing round the N. Ridge of Crib Goch and then striking up the screes, but by far the finest approach is to traverse the ridge. Leave baggage etc., on the top of the route and then descend from Bwlch Côch to the foot of the climb.

Parking at Pen Y Pass. Rescue facilities as for Dinas Cromlech.

The cliff is composed of a fine main buttress with a clearly defined R. hand edge, a central gully and then a more broken buttress, Crazy Pinnacle Buttress on the R.

Start immediately on the L. of the central gully by a 150 ft. slabby scramble to a stance overlooking the gully and at the foot of steeper rocks.

1   110 ft.   Climb directly up the rib to a large stance.

2   70 ft.   Climb L. with difficulty up the wall to a ledge below a fine pinnacle. Climb the pinnacle (runner!) and then make the famous stride across to the wall (crux). Follow a crack easing to another pinnacle top and a stance.

3   40 ft.   Continue direct up the rib above by a groove to finish very near the ridge.

A route on Lliwedd, followed by the Horseshoe and then this route gives a very fine mountaineering day.

143   G.W. Young's Climb. Clogwyn Pen Llechan. (Teyrn Bluffs.)

D+ 230 ft. Winthrop Young, Porter, 1913.
SE. Facing. 1,250 ft. above sea level. 200 ft. high.
G.R. 641545.
This crag and the next one lie below the Miners' Track between Pen Y Pass and Llyn Llydaw and on opposite sides of the pipe to Cwm Dyli. They give better climbing than one expects and are useful when bad weather makes Lliwedd unattractive.

They are easily reached from Pen Y Pass in 20 mins. and this is the first to be reached.

Parking at Pen Y Pass. Mountain Rescue facilities as for Dinas Cromlech.

The crag has two facets and the only decent route takes the junction of these up the SE. corner.

Start above a large quartz boulder.

1   40 ft.   Climb a short grassy chimney to a block on the L. which is gained with difficulty. Now traverse L. along a crack to a stance.

2   70 ft.   Take the slabs on the L. to reach a large block.

3 50 ft. Climb over the block to reach a terrace.
4 40 ft. Follow the terrace L. to a short, hard crack, then a series of ledges to a larger one.
5 30 ft. Follow the rib on the R. to the top.

144 Via Media. Craig Aderyn. (Teyrn Bluffs.)
VS— 160 ft.
SE. Facing. 1,250 ft. above sea-level. 150 ft. high.
G.R. 639543.
This is the companion to the previous crag and lies on the s. side of the pipeline. A variety of ways are possible up the smooth slabs of which this route is the finest. However, an M. up the R. edge, the Arête Climb, is also quite good.

Start at the centre of the slab.
1 100 ft. Take a direct line up the centre of the slab.
2 60 ft. Continue in the same line to join the arête.

C The Beddgelert Area

The climbs described in this area lie generally on the sides of the four valleys which radiate from the town of Beddgelert or the nearby village of Rhyd-ddu. To the E. lies the Gwynant Valley, low lying and green with s. facing crags, to the N. the Cwellyn Valley with the gentle side of Snowdon on the R. and Mynydd Mawr and Castell Cidwm on the L., to the w. the Pennant hills with Cwm Silin on the N. side and the sea-level Tremadoc crags at the s. whilst to the SE. the Moelwyns show their easier side.

Both Tremadoc and the Gwynant give quick drying small crag climbing of a wide variety of standard, although very little is suitable for the novice. Castell Cidwm is very different giving some of the steepest Welsh routes whilst Cwm Silin is a delightful high mountain area with something for everyone.

General facilities
Beddgelert provides the central point to stay for the area and is well equipped as a tourist resort.
(*i*) *Sleeping*
Hotels at Beddgelert and Tremadoc and the towns to the N., w. and s. of the area.
Guest houses at Beddgelert, Tremadoc, Rhyd Ddu, Pen Y Groes, Nant Gwynant and Waenfawr.

Plate 38. Clogwyn Y Wenallt

Farms with accommodation in all four valleys.

Accommodation bureau for Portmadoc 2327.

Youth Hostels at Bryn Gwynant and at Snowdon Ranger near Rhyd Ddu.

Barns at a farm at Tremadoc.

Climbing huts:

Tremadoc – Pant Ifan (569408) Cave and Crag.

Nant Gwynant, Cwm Dyli (652541) Pinnacle Club.

Rhyd Ddu, Tan Y Wyddfa (571527) Oread M.C.

Camp sites at Beddgelert (Forestry Commission site) and in the Gwynant (655528), at Hafod Y Rhisgl and Hafod Y Llan (628512).

Mountain centres at Plas Gwynant – West Bromwich L.E.A. and Aberglaslyn Hall – Leicestershire L.E.A.

(*ii*) *Eating*

Besides the usual meals at hotels, a cafe is open during the season in Beddgelert, whilst climbers at Tremadoc sometimes drive to the Cob Cafe in Portmadoc. (See also v.)

Shops for food at Beddgelert, Beryls Stores in Nant Gwynant, Tremadoc, Rhyd Ddu, etc. Early closing days, Beddgelert – Wednesday, Nant Gwynant – Wednesday, Tremadoc – Wednesday.

(*iii*) *Drinking*

Bars in all the hotels in the area. Climbers seem to favour the Union Inn in Tremadoc and the Quellyn Arms in Rhyd Ddu.

(*iv*) *Public Toilets*

At Beddgelert, Tremadoc and Rhyd Ddu.

(*v*) *Garages and Breakdown facilities*

Two garages with breakdown facilities at Beddgelert (Green's 260, Owen's 231).

A petrol station at Craig Bwlch Y Moch is notable for its other facilities which include parking, toilets, drinks and ices, etc., and some general supplies. A valuable asset to the area.

(*vi*) *Taxis and Hire Cars*

Taxis from Beddgelert 207, Portmadoc 2060 and Waenfawr 264. Car hire from Portmadoc 2475.

(*vii*) *Mountain Rescue*

The official post covering this area is at Aberglaslyn Hall (593459). In all cases, of rescue, ensure that police H.Q. (dial 999) is informed. Spare equipment is kept at the Quellyn Arms, Rhyd Ddu.

(*viii*) *Public 'Phone Boxes*

At Nant Gwynant, Beddgelert, Rhyd Ddu and Tremadoc, and Post Offices also.

Plate 39. Bovine pitch 4. The good holds arrive

Gwynant Valley. Clogwyn Y Wenallt
SE. Facing. 450 ft. above sea level. 250 ft. high.
G.R. 647527. Plate 38.

This fine crag lies in the Gwynant Valley above the
NE. end of Llyn Gwynant, and can be reached easily
via the bridge at the end of the lake and a short walk
up hill. 15 mins. from the old road.

Parking is usually possible in the field below the
crag whilst mountain rescue facilities exist at
Aberglaslyn Hall near Beddgelert.

The crag itself presents a broad, steep face cut by
a grassy terrace which comes in from the L. and fades
out in the centre. A wall and fence come up to meet
a large boulder at the foot of the crag and coupled
with the terrace gives sufficient landmarks for identi-
fying the starts of the routes. The routes are steep
and quite difficult but the rock is good, and in places,
the holds are immense. *Descents from this cliff are easy
via the grass slopes on the* L.

145 Bovine
*VS+ 220 ft. ** Davies, Wright, McKelvey, 1957.*
Just R. of the boulder and fence, one route, Shake
(vs) follows a line of cracks directly up the crag, but
the first really good route goes up the wall and a
steep groove above, about 15 yds. L. of the boulder.
This route, and a climb called Oxo (vs−) find ways
up this area of cliff, crossing at various points so it
is possible to vary them as Oxine or Bovox.

Start at a pointed boulder below a small gnarled
tree.

1 80 ft. Climb the wall to the tree, then go
slightly R. to a pinnacle. (Oxo reaches here by a
traverse and continues traversing to the R.) Above is
a steep corner which is climbed with the aid of a
piton to reach a flat ledge with belays to the L.

2 20 ft. The corner above is very awkward but
soon leads to a good grass terrace.

3 30 ft. Walk R. then climb easily down a slab
to a good stance and tree belay (Oxo traverse ends
here and it then goes up the slab and the steep crack
above the tree).

4 90 ft. A superb pitch. The steep wall above the
stance is cut initially by a short groove. Climb this
for a few ft. then make a hard move out R. onto
the face. The face is covered with good holds (**Plate**

39) and is climbed to the top with a short diversion to the R. before the final slab. (Oxo joins the last section by a traverse in from the L.)

146 Torero
HVS. 140 ft. * Brown, Whillans, 1959.

Oxo starts with a traverse a little to the L. of Bovine. 20 ft. L. again, a black wall leads up to a steep, clean corner. This excellent climb uses this groove to reach the grass terrace and then finds a hard way up the walls above it.

Start 40 ft. L. of Bovine, below a groove.

1 50 ft. Get into the corner from the L. and climb it to reach a good rock ledge. Climb the wall above moving R. to finish on a wide grass terrace.

2 50 ft. Above is an easy groove leading L. to a higher ledge. Go up this for a few ft. and then make a long step R. into a scoop on the face. Now use a sling placed precariously on a spike to the R. to reach small holds on the wall. A bold move R. leads to good holds and a small stance lies a few ft. higher.

3 40 ft. Climb the crack on the L. of the stance to reach easier ground, and so to the top of the crag.

147 Ferdinand
HVS+ 100 ft. * Brown, Jones, 1959.

This very hard route lies up a wall above the grass terrace on the L. of the crag. There is a pitch below the terrace, but the pitch described here is the only one of note.

Start on the large grass ledge at the foot of a corner containing oak trees, or climb a corner about 30 yds. from the stone wall to reach this point.

1 100 ft. Climb the corner for 10 ft., then move out across the wall into a fierce crack. Plenty of protection can be put into this crack, and great difficulty can be found in not using it for aid! However, awkward jamming is possible to reach a niche under the top overhang. This is comparatively easy and leads to a short crack and the top of the crag.

Tremadoc. Craig Bwlch Y Moch
S. Facing. 50 ft. above sea level. 200 ft. high. G.R. 577406.

This delightful crag is purely a rock climber's habitat, for it is divorced from real mountaineering. However, the weather is often good and the rock dries quickly, so it is always a very popular area. It lies above the A498 about 2 miles from Tremadoc and all routes can be reached from the road in times varying from 10 secs. to 3 mins.

Parking is possible at the petrol station below the L. end of the crag (also toilets and teas) and crag rescue facilities exist at Aberglaslyn Hall, although the local fire brigade has been known to 'have a go'.

The cliff has numerous routes of which all those above mild severe give good climbing. However, some are outstanding and these are described here. The rocks are divided by vegetated gullies into about ten buttresses and in late spring and summer some difficulty can be experienced in finding the starts of routes due to the forest below the crag. If the lines of Valerie's Rib (s+) which forms the L. end of the crag, Vector Buttress, a sheer R.-facing wall, and the two Slips, two grooves which limit the R. hand end of the main crag, are first located, then the other routes are less difficult to find. The climbing is very varied and usually surprisingly open once the tree tops are left.

148   The Grasper

*HVS+ 160 ft. ** Brown, Thomas, 1961.*
Valerie's Rib (s+) ascends the L. hand edge of the cliff while in its upper part, on the R., is a very steep wall, cut near the top by two grooves. This strenuous route climbs a lower wall to reach a small stance below the L. hand groove which it then takes to the top.

Start at a grass ledge about 100 ft. above the road and a few ft. L. of a steep corner crack (Clapton's Crack, vs).

1   90 ft.   Climb a short slab to a bulge and over this into a groove with holds on its R. From the top of this, step back L. to below an overhanging flake. Go round this to a foothold (very small) on a rib below more overhangs. Here a piton usually gives protection for the crux and a welcome rest before it. Move up into the overhang then layback out R. onto a good foothold. Now step back L. to a good crack and go up this to reach fine holds. A short traverse R. leads to a good stance and piton belay.
2   70 ft.   Climb over a little wall into the foot of the top groove (suspect runner on a large spike). Climb the groove using a piton early on and two

slings round the roof. From the final sling a bold move L. onto a rib gives a few desperate feet to the top.

For this, and the two following routes, the easiest descent is via the tree covered slopes on the L., finishing behind the farm. For all other routes, the gully just L. of Merlin gives the only practical way down the cliff. On no account should climbers cross the fields towards the churchyard.

149 Christmas Curry by Micah Finish

*S+ 260 ft. * Moulam, Barr, 1953.*

Midway between Valerie's Rib and Vector Buttress lies a slabby buttress, the R. arête of which is recognisable by a large overhang with a thin flake crack above it. This arête marks the line of the Plum, a delicate HVS whilst Christmas Curry starts below the arête but then climbs the face on the L., returning to the arête only for the last few ft. of the Micah Finish.

Start at an ivy covered chimney 90 ft. below the large overhang.

1   40 ft.   Climb the awkward chimney to a stance with many trees.

2   90 ft.   Traverse out onto the slabs on the L. and climb a pocketed crack line, first on the L., then on the R. to finally move L. to another tree covered ledge.

3   60 ft.   Climb the slab above over a small roof to reach more trees and another fine stance.

4   70 ft.   The normal finish now goes L. up walls and a scoop, but instead, go straight up behind the belay until a delicate traverse R. (crux) leads to the arête and good holds continue in a fine situation to the top.

150   The Fang

*HVS— 200 ft. ** Brown, Davies, 1961.*

This excellent and varied route climbs the prominent slab above the overhang with a fang-like spike in it. It lies mid-way between Christmas Curry and Vector Buttress.

Start in the gully below and R. of the fang (a VS+, Striptease, climbs the gully).

1   80 ft.   There is a small pinnacle just L. of the gully with a crack up its L. side. Climb this crack for a few ft., then step L. to a steep little corner. Up this with a good hold at the top to reach a ledge near vegetation. Next, traverse back R. past a

detached flake to reach a crack. Up this to a small stance and peg belay.

2   50 ft.   Climb the corner to reach a ring peg, and thread one rope through this. Step back down a little and traverse delicately out to the nose and round it to reach a slight ledge. Go up a few ft. to a small stance with chockstone belays.

3   70 ft.   Go out across the slab to the crest, then straight up on surprising holds to reach a ledge and so by an easy layback, final blocks and the top.

151   One Step in the Clouds

VS – *230 ft.* * *Jones, Moseley, 1958.*
Vector Buttress (**Plate 40**) is noticeable for the contrast of its large, overhanging R. hand face and its slabby L. hand side. This enjoyable route takes the slab side as near to the edge as possible.

Start at a corner below the L. side of the overhanging face.

1   30 ft.   Two cracks lead up to a tree.

2   60 ft.   From above the trees, go L. up the wall to reach a V-chimney. Climb this (hard) and so via easy rocks to a good stance.

3   90 ft.   Go round the corner then up the slabs passing near a grass ledge at 20 ft. (stance if required). Move out R. onto the lip of the overhangs past a small spike and continue delicately until a ledge leads L. to a tree stance.

4   70 ft.   Step back R. onto the face and make a hard move up to easier ground. Above, a diagonal crack goes out to the R. leading to the final stance.

152   Vector

ES – *250 ft.* *** *Brown, Davies, 1960. (Plate 40)*
This is one of the greatest of Welsh rock climbs, giving superb climbing on continually steep and usually overhanging rock. Masterly route finding and excellent protection make it a popular route for aspiring hard men.

Start below the main overhanging face behind a solitary tree.

1   60 ft.   Up a faint groove to reach a steep slab and via this a groove which leads to a pinnacle stance on the L.

2   80 ft.   A hard move R. to the foot of a crack gives promise of delights to come. The crack, once started, has good holds and leads to a little ledge

Plate 40. Vector on Bwlch Y Moch. One Step in the Clouds climbs the slabs to the L.

with a fine spike runner which takes at least a full weight sling. A precarious step goes out onto a slab (?) and two moves up this prove to be the hardest on the route. Above, a scimitar-like, ocre coloured slab, undercut and overhung, is climbed with a peg until it is possible (and desirable) to step L. to a fine foothold. A little groove, followed by a traverse with a piton finally brings the climber to a small, cramped cave in which he may hide for a while.

3 60 ft. Traverse L. below the overhangs, then swing over them on a good hold to reach a thin slab. Cross this to two pitons below a steep groove. This groove is strenuous and seems longer than its 15 ft. suggests, but it ends with quite good finishing holds and a stance on easy ground.

4 50 ft. Follow the easy part of the last pitch of One Step in the Clouds to the top.

153 Meshach

VS+ 200 ft. ** *James, Miss Earnshaw, Petrovsky, 1962.*

On the R. of Vector Buttress there is a vegetated gully and on the R. of this is an area of steep slabs with small high overhangs on the L., and a large pinnacle flake in the centre. This, and the following route, take these slabs and give good climbing whilst another VS+, Grim Wall, keeps well to the L. These slabs face a gateway on the road.

Start in trees below the centre of the slabs, reached by a scramble from the foot of Vector.

I 110 ft. Start up a slabby rake leading L. but leave this at the first break in the walls above at a sharp horizontal flake. A shallow chimney goes up to the upper slabs and after a few moves R., a traverse L. is made to a good ledge. Now straight up the slabs for 50 ft. until they become vertical (runner). Finally traverse L. with a last step down to a good stance.

2 90 ft. Climb straight up to the overhangs and turn them with difficulty. Move R. with a peg (**Plate 41**), then up on small holds to below the final wall. Step R. a few ft. and finish with a pull up on good holds to the top.

154 Shadrach

VS− 180 ft. ** *Moulam, Pigott, Thomas, 1951.*

This delightful classic route takes a fairly direct line

Plate 41. At the peg on Meshach

up the slabs on the R. of Meshach, via the large pinnacle flake.

Start a few ft. R. of Meshach. A large block has a steep crack on its L. and a gentler one on its R.

1 60 ft. Climb either crack to reach the top of the block. Fine belays.

2 50 ft. Traverse L. until a mantel-shelf leads to an upper slab. Go up this to a stance below the pinnacle.

3 70 ft. Crux. Either step off the top of the pinnacle and traverse L. into a niche (tall climbers) or step across low and use a rib to get into the niche (strong climbers). Now move up steeply until a slab goes out R. to the top.

155 Leg Slip

HVS — 210 ft. * Brown, Davies, 1960.
The R. hand edge of this area of rock is notable for two short grooves which cut its upper part. This climb, and a companion route, First Slip (ES—) ascend these grooves.

Start below the grooves at another groove capped by a large roof and containing trees.

1 40 ft. It is difficult to start the groove with clean feet, and quite hard to continue to the trees.

2 20 ft. Continue up the groove to a small tree below the roof. (First Slip goes R. from here and then thinly up the groove above with a piton.) Now step L. round the corner onto a slab leading to a tree stance in an easy angled groove.

3 65 ft. Climb the rake above, past an awkward corner to a V-chimney. Go up this a little, then make a hard move out R. and continue up to another tree belay

4 35 ft. Bridge the delicate groove above until another roof forces a bold move out L. Suddenly the climbing eases and a sheltered stance is reached.

5 50 ft. From the tree, reach a crack then slabs on the L.

156 Merlin

VS — 140 ft. Moulam, Jillott, 1956.
80 yds. further away from Tremadoc, opposite another gateway, lies a final, steep buttress which comes very near the road. This route takes a fairly good line up the buttress via a prominent flake crack above trees. Start about 40 ft. R. of the lowest rock

on boulders, below a very steep wall with a smooth slab on the R. (Y Broga, VS+, climbs the corner crack and continues up an arête.)

1   80 ft.   Climb the crack on the L. of the wall, turning an initial overhang with aid from a tree, and continuing up a corner to another overhang. Step out L. awkwardly onto easy slabs and up these to a big stance among trees.

2   40 ft.   One step up a slab gives access to a sharp edged crack which is climbed to reach a slab above on the R. Traverse this high using undercut holds to reach another tree stance.

3   20 ft.   Up the little corner to the top.

The face above the crack of pitch 2 gives a harder finish.

Tremadoc. Craig Pant Ifan

S. Facing. 200 ft. above sea level. 200 ft. high.
G.R. 571406.

This cliff is a little further from the road, a few hundred yds. nearer to Tremadoc village than Craig Bwlch Y Moch. It lies in a Nature Reserve, so only the correct approaches, which are marked, should be used. For the main buttress (Peuterey Buttress), the best approach is via a stile 70 yds. W. of the petrol station, whilst for Two-Face Buttress it is better to take the minor road out of Tremadoc, behind the Laundry, to its first corner (no parking) and then take a field path up and R.-wards on the edge of the woods until, after two more gates, it levels out and the top of the cliff is within reach. (This is the path leading to Pant Ifan, a climbing hut belonging to the Birmingham Cave and Crag Club.) The gully leading down to the foot of the crag faces, on the opposite side of the path, a minor cliff which gives some good little practice climbs.

Parking is possible at the aforementioned petrol station, and in Tremadoc village.

Cliff rescue facilities as for Craig Bwlch Y Moch.

As on Bwlch Y Moch, all the good climbing on this cliff is at Severe or above, and although vegetation is profuse below the crags, the rocks, particularly in their upper sections, are open and clean. The cliff is divided into three main sections by more vegetated areas and the routes selected lie on two of these. The central section, Peuterey Buttress, is steep and

Plate 42. Moving on to the nose on pitch 4 of Poor Man's Peuterey

smooth, presenting a main face of slabs topped by large, square overhangs, whilst well to the L. can be seen Two-Face Buttress which also is clean and slabby. The third main section, Hogmanay Buttress lies on the R. It is undercut, with upper grooves and walls. No routes are described on this section although a vs−, WOB, finds a way up well on the R. and semi-artificial routes climb its smooth central part.

157 Poor Man's Peuterey

S. 255 ft. * *Sutton, Gaukroger.*

The L. section of Peuterey Buttress is dominated by a large, overhanging tower of rock cut by a deep chimney. This route starts below the tower but avoids it by a traverse R. to reach and climb the upper layer of slabs. Enjoyable climbing with a good top section.

Start below a rib near a big tree, with a groove containing two hollies on the R.

1   55 ft.   Get on to the rib from the L. and climb it to a ledge with large trees.

2   40 ft.   Go into a groove on the R. and use this to reach more trees. (A deep chimney lies above, Strapiombo, HVS−, or a traverse L. for 40 ft. gives another finish, Pear Tree Variations, vs+.)

3   40 ft.   Traverse R. on vegetation to reach a small stance in more open surroundings. This stance is a fine view point. Great Western, vs, comes from the the R. up walls, a crack and a hard corner whilst Pincushion, an artificial climb, goes up the slab on the R. above the roof.

4   100 ft.   Up a slab to a piton in a horizontal crack. Use this crack to get out onto an exposed nose (**Plate 42**) and climb this to a ledge. Then take cracks in the slab above, first on the L. and later on the R. to a good stance above.

5   20 ft.   Climb up L. to a chimney and so to top.

Descend by going L. over the top of the crag until markers lead into a gully.

158 Barbarian

HVS. 240 ft. ** *Jones, Others, 1958.*

Just below and to the R. of the top pitch of Poor Man's Peuterey is a smooth slab above a long, square overhang, and topped by three, stepped overhangs. Up this slab goes Pincushion (HVS with 3 pegs).

Plate 43. Going R. at the bulge on pitch 1 of Helsinki Wall

To the R. of this is a steep corner with only(!) two of the three characteristic overhangs. It is here that this fine climb goes, usually one piton for protection and slight aid.

Start in the trees just below a little step in the path about 30 yds. R. of Poor Man's Peuterey, and directly below the corner.

1 50 ft. Up a little rib and past an arrow-headed block to reach the foot of the corner proper.

2 60 ft. Up near the corner with an interesting move when it steepens. Over this to a sitting stance and peg belay below the first overhang.

3 90 ft. Climb the overhang with difficulty and follow cracks in the slab to below the second overhang. Make a hard move out to stand in a niche with the feet in a horizontal crack. A piton is useful for balance now for the crux, a move round the nose L. into a wide crack. Up this to a stance.

4 40 ft. Move up R. into a corner then cross a slab to reach good holds and the finish.

159 Scratch Arête

*HVS— 200 ft. * Ingle, Jones, 1962.*

Scratch, VS, starts as for Barbarian but after one pitch escapes R. up slabs to find an easier line up the R. hand area of slabs. This route, as its name implies, climbs the arête on the R. of these slabs. Start about 15 ft. R. of the step in the path.A weakness leads to a T-shaped crack.

1 90 ft. Go up the rib tending R. to reach the foot of the crack. Climb it, quite interesting, then via a chimney on the L., get onto a final rib and so to a stance in trees below the arête. (The crux of Scratch, a layback corner, lies 20 ft. L. and traverses in to join the arête at the top.)

2 90 ft. Delicately up the slab to the overhang. Step R. onto a small ledge, then using a piton, get onto the upper slab. Climb this on good holds.

3 20 ft. Easily up the ridge to the top.

160 Helsinki Wall

*VS+ 140 ft. * Longland, Maden, 1955.*

A good route of continual interest, lying on the W. face of Two-Face Buttress. It can be seen easily from the path which descends to the foot of the crag.

Start 50 ft. below the wall at a thorn bush on mud.

1 60 ft. Climb the yellow rock for 30 ft. to a niche (piton protection). A bulge above makes moving R. rather committing and irreversible (**Plate 43**), but luckily a sloping ledge leads quickly to the arête and so to a good stance.

2 25 ft. Step down and traverse L. under overhangs until a stride over some blocks leads to a stance.

3 55 ft. Climb the groove behind the stance for some ft. to a piton and then step L. to another. Now go round the corner and jam and bridge up steep cracks until a final layback move finishes suddenly at the top.

161 Stromboli

HVS— 210 ft. ** Smith, Jones, 1956.

This route gives two pitches of great contrast, climbing the main face of Two-Face Buttress through its prominent overhangs.

Start on a little ledge 10 ft. down from the start of Helsinki Wall. Piton belay below large overhangs.

1 90 ft. Climb up the corner to the overhang and traverse R. onto the face. Cross a slab delicately and climb a short wall to a stance in trees. (This is also the start of Olympic Slab, vs, which then continues up a nice slab pitch above.)

2 40 ft. Scramble R. through trees to a stance below the large overhangs.

3 80 ft. A great pitch. Climb the slabs towards a wide chimney but avoid this by an exciting move L. on undercut holds in the roofs, until better holds allow the slab above to be gained. This slab leads to a second overhang which is turned via a V-chimney on the R. (a good place for losing nuts!). Hence to footholds below the final roof. A protective piton is usual here for the last move out into a groove on the R. (Every move gives surprising holds except one!)

Tremadoc. Craig Y Castell

S. Facing. 200 ft. above sea level. 200 ft. high.
G.R. 558404.

This cliff lies behind the school in Tremadoc village and can be seen well from the doorway of the Union Inn in the square. Usually it is reached by the fields on the L. of the school and then a direct approach up the screes in 10 mins.

Parking in the square or in the lane leading to the

school, but permission should be asked at the farm first, and access to the school and adjacent houses left well clear.

Crag rescues as for Bwlch Y Moch.

This cliff gives some of the best hard routes in the area plus one of the finest severes in Wales. The base of the cliff is hidden in trees but the main features are a L. hand area of steep slabs and a R. hand section of steep walls and square overhangs separated by a steep corner.

162   Creagh Dhu Wall

S+ 200 ft. *** *Cunningham, Smith, Vaughan, 1951.*
This great climb reaches the foot of the central corner via cracks below it and then goes out L. up the slabby nose.

Start below the central nose where a tree-filled weakness goes up to obvious cracks.

1   90 ft.   Easily up past trees, then better climbing in a groove and on the R. to reach an awkward slanting crack ending at a good runner. Now toe-traverse R. and go up to a good stance and belays just below the start of the upper corner.

2   80 ft.   A horizontal crack leads out L. onto the face of the slabs (**Plate 44**). Go up these in fine situations to a good ledge with belays 10 ft. above.

3   30 ft.   Move up L. to the foot of a groove and enter this with difficulty. Step up L. and finish on good holds.

It is difficult to select a crux on this route for although usually the move in the groove is found to be the hardest, the wrong technique used on the start of pitch 2 can produce problems for the climber (and amusement for the watchers!) *Descent is via a rocky traverse R. and then a steep tree filled weakness.*

163   Wasp

HVS+ 170 ft. * *Brown, Davies, 1960.*
This is the route up the prominent corner in the centre of the crag. It gives two fine pitches, the lower quite awkward, the upper superb friction bridging.

Start below reasonable slabs on the R. of the central section, at a grassy corner.

1   30 ft.   Climb up in the corner to a tree belay.

2   60 ft.   From the L. end of the ledge, get onto a pinnacle then climb the overhanging diagonal crack

Plate 44. Joe Brown on the slabs above the traversing crack on Creagh Dhu Wall

with the aid of two slings on chocks or nuts. (It is easy to use these too early).

3   80 ft.   From the L. end of the ledge, get into the bottom of the dièdre with aid from a threaded sling. A piton low and another at the overhang seem usual for the next section, then precarious backing up into a corner and a few final moves lead to a slab and the top.

A harder route, Pellagra (ES—) goes up the slabs on the R. of the corner and traverses under the final overhangs nearly into the corner before breaking out R. to finish. It starts up the corner above the first stance of Wasp.

164   Tensor
HVS. 260 ft. ** *Brown, Davies, 1964.*
Another hard climb finding a way through the overhangs on the R. of Pellagra and Wasp.

Start a few ft. R. of Wasp, below the slabs.

1   100 ft.   Climb the slab with a nice move at 60 ft. to a piton belay just above the level of the first line of overhangs. (This is pitch 1 of Tantallus, VS+, which continues up the buttress above with aid from one peg.)

2   100 ft.   Step with difficulty onto the slab and traverse across between the overhangs (**Plate 45**) until a groove leads through the upper one. Layback into and up this to a good foothold. Now make a hard move R. and up delicately to a peg under the roof. Using this and another above, climb the overhang to reach an easier groove and follow this to a small stance and piton belay.

3   60 ft.   Continue with less difficulty up the walls above.

Tremadoc. Craig Y Gesail
S. Facing. 250 ft. above sea level. 200 ft. high.
G.R. 545411.

This is the final crag in the area and lies to the w. of Tremadoc village, farther from the road than the other crags. It is reached by a narrow road going out of Penmorfa, and then by a walk past Tyddyn-dicwm Isaf, which lies below the cliffs. 15 mins. should suffice.

Cars can be parked in the narrow road provided they are pulled well over.

Plate 45. The traverse under the overhang on pitch 2 of Tensor

Mountain rescue as for Craig Bwlch Y Moch.

The climbing on this cliff is less serious than on the others, routes being shorter, not so steep, and separated by large vegetated areas. It is usually quieter than the other cliffs and the routes selected give good climbing. The main feature of the crag is a triangular area of slabs near the centre. To the R. of these is Midas Buttress, a clean, steep little wall with a pinnacle on its face. To the L. the crag is composed of separate buttresses rising out of the vegetation, of which Sheerline Buttress, next to the area of slabs, with a clean groove on its L. and the Castle, the last tower of rock to the w., are the most noticeable. Clutch goes up the clean groove, whilst the Castle gives a good vs+ starting in a gully on the R., but having a fine last pitch up the steep face above the overhangs.

165   Clutch

VS+. 130 ft. Moulam, Craster, Mawr, 1953.
This climb takes the groove on the L. of Sheerline Buttress. The main pitch is very good and the approach improves with wear!

Start up a tree filled gully until directly below the groove.

1   25 ft.   Climb up R. until an awkward move can be made onto a ledge, and follow this L. to a stance.
2   85 ft.   Go up cracks above to the foot of the groove and climb this with some difficulty. Suddenly it becomes too hard, so swing out onto the arête, and climb this to a good stance.
3   20 ft.   Climb the wall above on excellent holds.

166   Princess

S. 260 ft.   Harris, Neil, 1953.
This route starts up the lower slabs and then continues with nice, short pitches (all slightly artificial) up the buttress above.

Start a few ft. L. of a hollow at the foot of the slabs.
1   40 ft.   Go straight up to a large ledge in the middle of the slabs.
2   40 ft.   Delicately up the slabs then traverse R. to reach an easier groove below the overhangs.
3   50 ft.   Up to the overhangs, then up a non vegetated rib above.
4   30 ft.   Step out R. onto the face to a spike, then

R. again to a crack. Up this until an awkward step leads back L. to a stance.

5 40 ft. Go up to twin cracks and climb the L. one. Tree belays.

6 60 ft. Traverse delicately R. onto the arête, then mantel-shelf into a corner. Up this to the top.

167 Touch and Go

*VS+. 120 ft. * James, Benson, 1957.*

The easiest descents from the top of the crag go down grass at either end. That on the R. goes down a little rake from which the profile of Midas Buttress can be seen well, with its pinnacle quite prominent. This route reaches a ledge on the L. of the pinnacle and then uses that to finish

Start below an overhung V-chimney below the pinnacle.

1 20 ft. Scramble up a slab to below the chimney.

2 45 ft. Climb the chimney to the roof, then step out L. Toe traverse delicately to a stance round the corner.

3 10 ft. Up to the next ledge.

4 45 ft. Crux. Mantel-shelf out onto a ledge on the face, then climb the pinnacle. Make a step up onto the wall above and so to the top.

Mynydd Mawr. Castell Cidwm

SE. Facing. 750 ft. above sea level. 200 ft. high.
G.R. 550553. Plate 46.

This isolated mountain has climbing faces on three sides. To the s., above the B4418 lies Craig y Bera, a shattered wall of cliffs giving a loose D, Sentries Ridge on the R., and an s. Angel Pavement (181) up slabs in the centre. To the N., Craig Cwm Du gives an s+ Adam Rib. However, to the E., a stream cuts into the mountain from the shore of Llyn Cwellyn, and Castell Cidwm is the cliff which forms the N. bank of this stream. Legally, it can only be approached from the southern end of the lake via a forestry commission road (no vehicles allowed). The pleasant walk takes about 30 mins.

Parking is possible at the farm at the start of this road (G.R. 568539), after gaining permission from the farmer. Otherwise in Rhyd Ddu village.

Mountain rescue facilities are at Aberglaslyn Hall, although equipment is kept also at Quellyn Arms in Rhyd Ddu.

Plate 46. Castell Cidwm

The main section of the crag is composed of a 200 ft. face rising from two terraces 100 ft. above the stream. It can be seen, and climbing watched from the grass banks opposite. On the far L. it is bounded by a corner with a line of overhangs extending 70 ft. towards the centre. This is a smoother area with many small (and not so small) overhangs dotted about it. Then on the R. is a great, sloping, square overhang with a final very overhanging wall tailing off in a faint gully. This gully is the upper section of the R-hand terrace which is reached from directly below, whilst the horizontal, grassy L. hand terrace is reached from the L. by a short traverse.

The crag is one of the steepest and finest in Wales, giving routes of high standard of difficulty. Protection is usually by piton or nuts, for the holds are rather flat.

168   The Curver
HVS−. 180 ft. * Brown, Jones, 1960.
This is the easiest route on the face, yet it is still very serious, giving a taste of the considerable exposure which all the routes have. It uses the L. corner and breaks through the roofs at their smallest.

Start in the middle of the L. hand terrace, below start of a gangway.

1   60 ft.   Climb up a little, then follow the gangway R. to a niche with a piton belay.

2   120 ft.   Continue the traverse with overhangs above and below (**Plate 47**), making a long stride past a bulge then along a ledge to a piton. Step with difficulty round into a small corner and climb this to the top. Care is needed on this pitch to avoid excessive rope drag.

Descent from all routes via the grass slopes to the L. of the cliff.

169   Central Wall
ES− 180 ft. ** Clements and Bell, 1964.
A tremendous route up the very steep central section of the cliff. The climbing is continually steep and serious with protection hard to get and only a little aid from pegs.

Start in the middle of the L. hand terrace, below a clean v groove which leans to the R. Belay!

1   80 ft.   Up easily to the foot of the groove and climb this to an awkward landing on the L. (peg runner). Climb with difficulty up the wall on the L.

Plate 47. Between the overhangs on Curver

to a scoop below the overhangs. Turn these on the
L. with two pegs for aid, then step L. to a small stance
and peg belay.

2   100 ft.   Go L. for 5 ft., then diagonally R. to a
roof. Over this on large holds and continue up the
steep groove above to a piton below a wall. Climb
the wall to the top of the crag.

The girdle traverse of this cliff is one of the hardest
climbs in Wales (ES). It descends much of pitch 2
before continuing across very steep rock to reach
finally the traverse of Curver and to descend this.

170   Vertigo
HVS— 120 ft. ** *Brown, Wright, 1960.*
This superbly exposed climb takes a steep line up
the R. side of the central wall. The climbing is much
less difficult than one would expect, with enough
protection to allow full enjoyment.

Start near the R. end of the terrace below and to
the L. of black slabs which are 20 ft. R. of the central
wall.

1   60 ft.   Climb the slabs without great difficulty to
a steepening at 15 ft. Step L., then R.-wards up a
scoop with footholds on a shattered overhang on the
R., to reach a peg. Bridge up by this until a move
can be made to a ledge on the R. Traverse easily
15 ft. R. to a good stance and peg belay.

2   60 ft.   Step round the arête (**Plate 48**) to reach
a steep crack which is climbed direct to the bulges
above. Finally, dodge an uninteresting loose
chimney by a delightful 15 ft. traverse R.

171   Dwm
HVS— 180 ft. * *Brown, Jones, 1960.*
Despite its foreboding name, this is a very enjoyable
climb round the large, square overhang on the R. of
the crag. It is mostly free climbing with an artificial
section under the roof.

Start on the R. hand terrace, below a groove
which leads up to the roof.

1   60 ft.   Climb onto a large block from the R.,
and swing across a steep wall to a niche. Now climb
up steeply on good holds and get across to a crack on
the R. Follow this to a good stance with peg belay.

2   60 ft.   Go up the overhanging wall on the L. of
the ledge to another ledge (peg), then traverse
diagonally R., first on side pulls and then finally

Plate 48. Starting the second pitch of Vertigo

Plate 49. Cwm Silin. Craig Yr Ogof

by a delicate traverse on a black ledge to the groove below the overhang. Peg belays.

3   60 ft.   Go up the corner to the roof, traverse under it with pitons, and continue up an easy bottomless chimney to the top.

One of the most strenuous routes in Wales climbs the overhangs on the R. of Dwm using two pegs (one early) and slings at both roofs to follow the line of the crack which cuts them. This is Tramgo(ES−).

Cwm Silin
N. Facing. 1,750 ft. above sea-level. 300 ft. high.
G.R. 517501. **Plate 49.**

This fine crag lies in the hills to the s. of the Nantlle Valley and above Llynnau Cwm Silin. The crag is reached by following a narrow road towards Llan-llyfni which branches off the Nantlle-Tal Y Sarn road. About a mile along this, a lane leads L. just past Tan-Yr-Allt (G.R. 481521) to the farm of Bryn Gwyn. From here a grass track continues across the fields through three locked gates to the cwm itself, whence the routes can be approached direct up the screes. About 45 mins. from the car.

Parking is possible in the fields before the first locked gate.

Mountain rescue facilities as for Mynydd Mawr.

All the routes except one lie on the big central cliff above the lake and known as Craig Yr Ogof. This is a simple crag composed of a 300 ft. w.-facing slab, Great Slab, and at right-angles to this, a very steep front face with a shallow cave at half height. The odd route, Overhanging Chimney, lies on Trwyn Y Graig which is a smaller, separate crag lying well to the E. above twin marshy lakes and is *not* the crag next to Craig Yr Ogof.

The climbing varies considerably with the section of crags on which it is found; on the slab, delightful and often very easy; on the nose, very steep and exposed; and on Trwyn Y Graig, up a succession of fine chimneys. Better weather and less crowds make this a strong rival to the more popular climbing areas in Snowdonia.

172   Overhanging Chimneys − Trwyn Y Craig
VD+ 310 ft. Downes, Carr, McNaught, 1926.
A route of character and continual interest. Well worth the walk!

Start at the foot of the lowest section of the crag, below a high, prominent nose.

1 60 ft. Climb up to a flake (runner) on a terrace then up the wall above to reach a broad heather ledge. Cross this to a belay.

2 60 ft. Up the slab on the R. on small holds to a hard crack (Maurice's Crack). Up this until a traverse L. leads to a stance.

3 40 ft. Climb the first overhanging chimney.

4 45 ft. Now take a good crack up the steep wall.

5 30 ft. Climb the next overhanging chimney to a ledge below the nose.

6 55 ft. Climb up on the R. (by a slab) of the nose to a sloping ledge. Then swing out R. to the third overhanging chimney. Up this.

7 20 ft. Ignore the easy chimney and climb the steep crack on the L. to the top.

173 Ogof Direct – Craig Yr Ogof

*HVS. 280 ft. * Moulam, Pigott, Bowman, 1952.*

As its name implies, this excellent route reaches the Ogof from below then finds a way up the steep wall above it. Approaches to the cave are not hard but the upper section with the direct finish described gives some very exciting climbing.

Start at the very tip of the buttress at a small crack leading up to a nose.

1 25 ft. Up to a spike, then L. to a ledge by the nose.

2 80 ft. Onto the nose and follow it to a corner. Up this to a belay.

3 30 ft. Up slabs again to the Ogof.

The warming up section of VD standard is now over, and the real problem begins.

4 75 ft. From a piton belay on the L. of the cave, climb grooves and ribs to an overhang. There is a sloping ledge on the R. which can be gained with aid from a threaded sling (or a peg). Now take a thin diagonal crack R.-wards (sometimes a peg at 10 ft.) up difficult rock to a grass ledge below more roofs.

5 25 ft. It is possible to traverse R. here and after one difficult move, to reach easy ground and so follow the Outside Edge Route (175) to the top. Instead, however, climb the overhanging corner crack above with the aid of a peg to a small stance and peg belay.

6   45 ft.   Climb the corner on the R., then go further R. to join the Outside Edge Route just before its last pitch. Continue up this (175).

To descent go well R. to a scree gully and down keeping R.

174   The Crucible – Craig Yr Ogof

*HVS. 300 ft. *** Ingle, Wilson, 1963.*

Between the Ogof and the Great Slab lies a very steep wall made up of steep grooves and overhangs. High on its L. side lies a great roof which this magnificent route reaches by a diagonal line from below, and turns on the R. Wonderful climbing, never really hard but always exposed and interesting make this one of the best climbs in Wales.

Start about 40 ft. L. of the Great Slab, at the foot of a groove, the centre one of three.

1   60 ft.   Go easily up the groove and at the first overhang step R., go up, and then move back L. onto the nose above. Make a long step L. to a stance and piton belay.

2   40 ft.   Step across L., then go pleasantly up a slab to a steepening. Move R. onto holds above a roof and so reach another delightful stance. Awkward thread belays or a peg for the impatient.

3   80 ft.   There is a perched block on the L. Move slightly down across this and so up into a little corner under an overhang. Get up to the roof and over it with aid of a peg to reach a sloping ledge (crux). Traverse L. into a groove (runner) then low again across a very steep wall to reach a crack and a cramped stance and chockstone belay. A good pitch needing a steady second also.

4   120 ft.   Climb the groove for a few ft., then a rib on the L. until an exciting move can be made back into the corner which is followed past a bulge to a resting ledge. It is worth fixing a good runner here! Now go out R. onto a slab. Up this very delicately to the large roof. Some holds here seem suspect but they are good enough to allow a breath holding move to be made down R. and round into an odd little niche. This niche is as untenable as the slab, so step R. again with fine holds to below a slabby groove. Up this, interesting, to grass and the large stance below pitch 4 of the Outside Edge Route.

A short traverse R. leads to the Ordinary Route which can be descended, solo, to save wear to PA's and toes on the normal descent!

Plate 50. On Cwm Silin. Great Slab

175   Great Slab. Outside Edge – Craig Yr Ogof

VD. 250 ft. ** **w** *Edwards, Palmer, 1931.*

This fine slab has various routes up it and in fact, although steep, has excellent holds and a fair number of weaknesses. The Ordinary Route (**Plate 50**), a pleasant D –, takes a diagonal line from low on the R. up to the top L. ridge with a little awkward wall at about 40 ft. on the first pitch, and then quite easy climbing moving across the slab and up slight chimneys, etc. It has large holds, short pitches and good stances and belays. However, this route, which follows the L. edge of the slab, gives good steep climbing with fine holds (although smaller) and small stances.

Start about 20 ft. in from the edge, below a slight cave.

1   **60 ft.**   Climb a sloping groove to the cave, and leave this on the R. to reach a stance a little higher.

2   **40 ft.**   Go steeply up the wall on the L. with running belays until a traverse L. leads to another good stance near the edge.

3   **40 ft.**   Climb the arête to a stance on a grass ledge just round the corner on the L. (The Ordinary Route comes in here and continues up an open chimney above).

4   **50 ft.**   Go 20 ft. L. to a grass corner and a slab leading up to a rib. High belay. Traverse L. low down over this rib to another, which is used to reach a grassy stance above a grass ledge.

5   **60 ft.**   Climb L. to the foot of a grassy crack and follow this to the ridge.

This is followed easily to the top of the crag in about 100 ft.

176   Kirkus' Route – Craig Yr Ogof

VS. 310 ft. * *Kirkus, MacFee, 1931.*

On the R. of the Great Slab is a waterworn groove. This delightful climb takes a line up the slab parallel to the groove and about 40 ft. out on the slab.

Start 15 ft. in from the line of the groove (Ordinary Route starts 40 ft. to the L.).

1   **90 ft.**   Climb the wet slab to an overhang and go round this on the L. to reach a traversing line. Follow this L. for 20 ft. until holds lead up to a diagonal crack. Get into this and follow it delicately until it levels and leads round the corner to the R.

to a niche. It is difficult to protect the second from this stance so continue steeply for 20 ft. to a stance on piled blocks.

2 60 ft. Climb delicately L. across a groove to follow small holds up to a staircase. This leads L. to a small stance with running belays. From the runner, step L. to reach a slab on the L. and a grass ledge.

3 70 ft. Climb diagonally R. up a smooth slab until a nice move over a little overhang leads up to another grass ledge.

4 50 ft. Climb the slab on the L. of a grass rake to another stance.

5 40 ft. A crack, followed by a high step L., leads to easy climbing and the top.

Beddgelert Area. Outlying Climbs

177 Lockwood's Chimney. Clogwyn Y Bustach

D+ 580 ft. including walking * **w** *Lockwood, 1909. SE. Facing. 500 ft. above sea level. 200 ft. high + lower cliffs. G.R. 650532.*

Clogwyn Y Bustach is a large broken, tree covered crag on the E. flank of Gallt Y Wenallt. It is reached in under ½ hr. by the path which starts behind Cwm Dyli Power Station and which follows the w. bank of the Afon Glaslyn and enters the woods below the cliff.

Parking is not allowed at the power station, so cars must be left in laybys on the old or new roads.

Mountain Rescue facilities as for Clogwyn Y Wenallt.

The crag is divided in two by a large tree filled gully (N. Gully) and to the R. of this lies North Buttress with smooth slabs and overhangs. However, our route is the route of the crag and as it starts well down in the woods, knowledge of the topography of the crag is superfluous and indeed removes some of the fun.

Start by following the valley track until a hill on the L. cuts out the view of the river just after a large wet overhanging boulder. Go up L. through the woods until a grassy bluff (house size) with a cave on its L. side is reached. A cairn marks the start of the climbing and the end of the orienteering.

1 90 ft. Start on the L. and go straight up to a large area of grass. Now take a green corner and a traverse R. to the nose which is followed to the top of the bluff.

2   100 ft.   From the top of the bluff continue over a secondary block and then walk up R. through the forest to the main arête. (*The descent path comes down to here from the L. so sacks may now be left.* This point may be arrived at in mistake for the correct start if too steep a line is taken up from the path.)

3   100 ft.   Climb direct up the arête, quite hard, until good pockets lead to easier rock and a ledge below a large block. Go over it to a crevassed stance.

4   70 ft.   Go up L. to the Marble Arch and pass this either over it from R. to L. or via a hole on the L.

5   60 ft.   Descend a little and follow an easy rising traverse to the foot of a black crack with a tree in it.

6   20 ft.   Climb the crack, the crux, to the foot of the chimney proper.

7   100 ft.   Enter the crack behind the belay, which leads to the chimney. Now struggle up this over a chockstone and then sidle along the floor until holds lead up round a corner and out onto a fabulous stance on the face. A surprising arrival.

8   40 ft.   Easy climbing in fine position to the top of the crag.   Various routes climb the steep walls to the L. of the chimney, but all are inferior to the chimney. *Descend to the L.*

178   Aquila. Craig Y Llyn

HVS— 200 ft. Banner, Neill, 1955.
E. Facing crag. 500 ft. above sea level. 250 ft. high.
G.R. 620501.

This steep, unattractive looking crag lies above the road at the W. end of Llyn Dinas. In general the climbing is poor, vegetated and loose, but on the steepest face, just L. of a large central depression, are to be found two better routes. Peachpla, a VS+, goes up just L. of the central nose giving steep climbing first up a sloping gangway and then up walls broken by ledges. The selected route takes the R. part of this face, giving varied climbing.

Start at the foot of a rib which comes down from the steepest part of the wall. Scramble up to this.

1   100 ft.   The rib is reached from the R. and can be climbed with difficulty up mossy slabs to reach a crack. Continue up this to a stance by a large block below the steepest wall.

2   30 ft.   An awkward traverse R. on grass ledges

Plate 51. Pitch 2 of Hardd. Just above the peg

to a block stance below the crux.

3   30 ft.   The wall above is very steep but with holds. Climb it, bold, and when all seems desperate, step R. round a corner into a cracked groove. Climb this to a fine stance.

4   40 ft.   First a pleasant chimney, then an awkward crack on the L. lead to good holds and the top.

Descent by a gully on the L. of the crag.

179   Hardd. Carreg Hyll-Drem

HVS. 230 ft. ** *Brown, Roberts, Drasdo, 1960.*
SE. Facing crag. 50 ft. above sea level. 200 ft. high.
G.R. 615431.

This excellent crag (for the hard man) lies on the Aberglaslyn-Penrhyndeudraeth road (A487), 3 miles from Beddgelert. It has about six routes up it, of which this route and a low girdle give the best climbing.

Parking is possible on the road below the crag and mountain rescue facilities are available at Aberglaslyn Hall.

The main section of the crag is overhanging with a wall on the R. above gentle slabs, which rise from an oak tree at the foot. Hardd climbs this wall whilst the Girdle (HVS −) starts at the tree and goes L. between the lower bulges and the large overhangs.

Start at the tree below the highest part of the crag.

1   60 ft.   From the tree go up R. on the slabs past a cave to a slabby stance. Peg belay.

2   60 ft.   Move up above the stance and then L. onto a steep wall. Climb a crack to a good peg and so using this reach a sloping hold below very steep walls. (**Plate 51**). Difficult moves to the L. on poor holds lead to a resting place below a bulge. Go over this and layback round the bulge above to arrive at a sloping stance with various peg belays. A toe crushing stance, but welcome!

3   60 ft.   Step across low and L. to a groove and up this to a flat ledge with a piton. Direct finish, HVS+, is directly above with a sling and a peg for aid. However, ignore this and abseil 15 ft. down an overhanging groove until a hand traverse leads L. with footholds arriving. (Skill at rope moves or plenty of rope seem advisable for this section.) Now go more easily to a good, exposed stance.

4   50 ft.   Easier climbing up a loose groove above.

Descend via grass and woods well to the R. of the crag.

180   Eastern Arête. Nantlle Y Garn

S— 330 ft. * Heskett-Smith, 1904.
N. Facing crag. 1,700 ft. above sea level. 300 ft. high.
G.R. 551527.

This climb takes, in fact, the NE. arête of the Nantlle
Y Garn high above Bwlch Gylfin. It is possible to
approach the crag direct from the bwlch, although
there are, at present, access problems on this route.
Therefore, it may be better to start from lower down
the Pass on the Rhyd Ddu side near the farm of
Drws Y Coed just above Llyn Y Gadair. Either way
takes over 30 mins. Alternatively a route on Craig
Cwm Silyn followed by the walk along the ridge
brings one to the top of the crag from whence the
route can be easily reached.

Parking is possible at Rhyd Ddu and on the road
above, and mountain rescue facilities are as for
Castell Cidwm.

The topography is simple, two buttresses separated
by *a central gully – the descent route.* The R. hand crag
gives a s route, Central Ridge, whilst our climb takes
the crest of the L. hand buttress.

Start at the edge of the buttress, just before the
scree and grass of the gully, about 70 yds. R. of a
dry stone wall.

1   100 ft.   Climb a short chimney to reach the
edge and then grooves to reach a stance below a nose.
2   30 ft.   Climb the nose on small holds to a
sloping ledge, the Study.
3   70 ft.   Climb the corner on peculiar holds, then
easily to another stance.
4   30 ft.   The crack on the R. is difficult.
5   100 ft.   Climb easily up the edge until a step R.
leads to the foot of a final chimney. Up this to the
top.

181   Angel Pavement. Craig Y Bera

S. 480 ft. * Brown, Moulam, 1946.
S. Facing. 1,400 ft. above sea level, 400 ft. high.
G.R. 545541.

This large crag is composed (or decomposed!) of
numerous totty ridges. However, one area, the
buttress which meets the dry stone wall from Drws
Y Coed, is generally on firmer rock and gives an
easy route, Pinnacle Ridge D, up its R. edge and this
climb up the centre. Further R. can be found Sentries
Ridge (D—) if it hasn't fallen down yet; it lies up

the second ridge from the R. hand end of the crag,
and involves the ascent of over a dozen pinnacles.

The shortest approach to the cliff is from straight
below, up the stone wall, but this is at present not
permitted by the farmer and so it is preferable to
take the official marked path up Mynydd Mawr
starting from Planwydd (GR 568539) at the head of
Llyn Quellyn, and then contour round to the foot of
the cliff.

Start at the centre of the slab about 30 yds. L. of
the wall.

1   **140 ft.**   Straight up the slab to a good stance.
2   **140 ft.**   The slab above a little wall is climbed
to a stance and thread belays below an overhang.
3   **50 ft.**   Climb with difficulty up the narrow slab
(crux).
4   **50 ft.**   Vegetated and less pleasant climbing to
a grass ledge.
5   **100 ft.**   Keep moving L. below very steep rock
to reach good ledges.
6   Scrambling over pinnacles, etc. (loose) to the top.

A good continuation to this route is to traverse
the mountain and to descend N. and then w. into
Cwm Bychan Cwm Du where Adam Rib (s+) on
Craig Cwm Du gives a fine second climb. It takes the
clean cut rib just L. of the columnar buttress on the
L. of the crag.

D   Dolwyddelan Area

This rather spread out area covers the climbing on
the E. side of Snowdonia, usually accessible from the
A496 road. The routes in Cwm Penamnen and
Crafnant are small steep climbs on sunny crags,
whilst the Meolwyns give a mountain type of climbing. Generally the routes typify the 'modern' style
although some of the longer climbs are of pre-war
origin.

General facilities
Dolwyddelan and Betws Y Coed are both tourist
resorts and so as well as those facilities expected by
the visiting climber they also provide many other
services (Welsh Home Craft shops, etc.!)
(*i*) *Sleeping*
Hotels at Betws Y Coed, Dolwyddelan, Blaenau
Ffestiniog and Llanrwst. Guesthouses also.

Farms with accommodation between Betws and Dolwyddelan and around Betws Y Coed.

Youth Hostels at Llanrwst (Oaklands), Dolwyddelan (Lledr House) and Ffestiniog.

Climbing huts: Liverpool and District M.C. at Tan Y Grisiau (684452).

Bangor University at Tan Y Grisiau (680461)

Mynydd M.C. Blaen Y Nant at Crafnant (738602).

Camp sites are frequent around Betws Y Coed and near Dolwyddelan.

Mountain Centres at Dolwyddelan – Plas, Tube Investments, and at Ffestiniog, Plas Dol Y Moch (684418) Coventry L.E.A.

(*ii*) *Eating*

Meals at most of the hotels, plus cafes in Betws Y Coed. Shops in all the towns. Early closing days, Llanrwst – Thursday, Bettws Y Coed – Thursday, Dolwyddelan – Wednesday/Thursday, Blaenau Ffestiniog – Thursday.

(*iii*) *Drinking*

Llanrwst hotels and some of the hotels up the hill on the A5 out of Betws Y Coed towards England, open on Sundays, otherwise most hotels have bars. The Waterloo Hotel, Bettws Y Coed may become popular with climbers. Licensing hours
11.30–3.00, 6.00–10.30 p.m.

(*iv*) *Public toilets in all the towns.*

(*v*) *Garages and Breakdown facilities.*

At Llanrwst (Central Garage 445 and Kerry Garage Garage 381), at Betws Y Coed (Betws Y Coed Motors, 303) and at Blaenau Ffestiniog (Cambrian Motors, 211). Petrol pumps at Tal Y Bont, Trefriw, and Dolwyddelan also.

(*vi*) *Bus Services, Taxis and Hire Cars.*

Regular bus services between Llanrwst and Blaenau Ffestiniog. Taxis available from Penmachno 209, Pentrefoelas 244 and Llanrwst 640226. Car hire at Penrhyndeudraeth 384.

(*vii*) *Mountain rescue*

Official posts for the area are Plas Y Brenin (Capel Curig 214) for the N. part and Blaenau Ffestiniog Police (252) for the Moelwyns. Please inform the Police (dial 999) of all rescue call outs. Help may often be obtained from Plas T.I. at Pont Y Pant (Dolwyddelan 206) and Plas Dol Y Moch Adventure School (Ffestiniog 623).

(*viii*) *Public 'Phone Boxes*

Plate 52. Starting the groove on Penamnan Groove. Lightning Visit takes the groove to the L.

These can be found in all towns and villages, Post offices at Betws Y Coed, Llanrwst and Blaenau Ffestiniog.

Cwm Penamnan. Carreg Alltrem

W. Facing. 1,000 ft. above sea level. 200 ft. high.
G.R. 739507.

This fine little crag lies in the quiet cwm which runs s. from Dolwyddelan. It is approached by the track from Dolwyddelan (passable for cars) until opposite the crag, whence a forestry break leads, via an old collapsed bridge, directly to the rock in ten mins.

Approach is sometimes possible via a forestry road under the crag.

The nearest official mountain rescue post is Plas Y Brenin, Capel Curig, although equipment and very skilled help can be obtained usually from Plas T.I. Mountain Centre at Pont Y Pant (G.R. 756538).

The topography of the cliff is quite simple, with the routes being orientated by the position of the great central overhung groove. All the routes are steep with fine holds and in good situations.

182   Penamnan Groove

*HVS+ 130 ft. * Downes: Miss Clark, 1956.*
This hard route takes the central groove and finds an interesting way through the overhangs above. The arête on the L. of this line is divided by a shallow, curing groove which is Lightning Visit (vs) whilst the wall to the L. of that has two or three routes up it, of which Fratricide Wall (vs+), just next to Lightning Visit, is the best.

Start directly below the main groove on a steep corner, often wet

1   45 ft.   Climb the corner (hard) to large ledge and fine belays.

2   85 ft.   Step up to the foot of the crack (**Plate 52**) and jam or layback (!) to the overhang. It is possible to fit runners on chockstones in the crack but this tiring process usually makes it then necessary to use them for aid. At the overhang, hang a short sling on a spike on the L. wall and use this for aid to get into the chimney above. Up this, and a groove above to the top.
Descent down a gully well to the R.

183 Lavaredo

*VS. 145 ft. ** James, Forder, Campbell, 1961.*
This climb lies up the steep wall on the R. of
Penamnan Groove and its attractions lie in the
position and holds of the second pitch.

Start 30 ft. R. of Penamnan Groove where a crack
and a groove run up either side of a detached finger.

1   75 ft.   Climb the R. hand groove for 30 ft. to a
flake on the R., step L. awkwardly onto a ledge and
continue to a grassy ledge and block belay.

2   70 ft.   Get up a wide crack on the L. to a large
block and then step L. immediately onto steep rock
and so go up on small holds until a move R. is
possible. Now go up on better holds until a semi
hand-traverse L. leads to an open corner and the top.
Many runners.

Moelwyn Crags

*Generally SE. Facing. 1,200 ft. above sea level. 200–400 ft.
high*

This section is made up of routes lying on the line of
crags which start above the village of Tan Y Grisiau
and run sw. above the new lake. The routes selected
lie on four crags, all of which are best approached
from a parking place on the quarry track to Llyn
Cwmorthin (GR 683455). A new road runs up
below the three L. hand crags although its owners do
not permit climbers to use it with vehicles, but it can
be reached on foot by a short traverse from the car
park.

Mountain rescue equipment is kept at Blaenau
Ffestiniog Police Station and there are telephones at
Llyn Stwlan dam and in Tan Y Grisiau village.

Craig Nyth y Gigfan is the most easterly of the
cliffs, lying high on the R. of the quarry track. It can
be reached up this and then via slate tips, in 30 mins.,
whilst the other obvious crag seen from the car park
is Craig Yr Wrysgan, a large slabby face high on the
L. of the stream with a quarry incline on its L. Craig
Yr Oen is visible also from the car park, forming the
L hand skyline of the crags with Kirkus' Route
actually following the arête. When walking up the
road this crag lies just past a stream at the levelling
of the road. Finally, Clogwyn Y Bustach, lies just
round the corner out of sight, and is the next steep

crag up the road. All can be reached in under
30 mins.

The rock on these cliffs is generally sound, although
sometimes a little mossy. Holds are often pocketed
incuts and protection is usually possible, although a
little ingenuity helps. Power stations and pylons
spoil the view, but one still finds a wildness here
which is missing in the more crowded areas.

184 Asahel
*S+ 160 ft. * James, Roberts, 1955.*
Craig Nyth Y Gigfan (GR 685458) is a steep crag,
divided by a shallow easy central depression, into two
buttresses, one facing sw. and one facing se. An old
wall joining the quarry track to the crag marks the
edge of this depression. On the L. buttress various
weaknesses give routes of around D/VD standard,
whilst its R. edge gives Thin Wall Special (vs).
However, both described routes lie on the bigger, R.
buttress which is notable for a quartz slab (White
Slab) on the L. and steep corners well to the R. This
climb takes the inside corner of the White Slab and
turns the overhangs with a traverse onto the arête of
the slab. Incidentally, the slab has many other lines
on it of which Africa Rib (VD) up its L. edge is the
best.

Start below the R. corner of the slab.

1   100 ft.   Up the slabs keeping near the corner
and turning a little bulge at 70 ft. by a traverse R.
and then back L. to a small stance.

2   40 ft.   Continue up the corner (thin) and traverse L. just below the overhangs to reach a rib. Up
this to a large stance.

3   20 ft.   Step round the corner R. and climb a wall
to the top.

The way off lies to the L. across slabs to a grassy funnel.

185 Mean Feet
*HVS. 130 ft. ** James, Vaughan, 1957.*
On the R. of the White Slab lies an area of very
steep rock cut, high up, by an overhanging V-chimney.
The route reaches this chimney from the R. by a
long rising traverse.

Start well to the R. below a vegetated corner.
(Double Chris, vs+, goes up the edge of this corner
and the overhanging crack above).

1   20 ft.   Scramble up into the corner.

2   50 ft.   Go up a short crack on the L., then make a semi hand-traverse diagonally L. for 40 ft. to a niche. Step L. again to a stance and chock belay at the foot of the V-chimney.

3   30 ft.   Climb the V-chimney (crux) (**Plate 53**).

4   30 ft.   The wall on the R. is harder than it looks.

186   Y Gelynen

VD+ 310 ft. ** *Davies, Williams, 1953.*

Craig Yr Wrysgan (GR 679454) is a large crag extending from the quarry incline on its L. with its associated tunnel to the stream falling from Cwm Orthin on the R. Many routes and variations are possible up the many ribs and corners, whilst the horizontal grass ledges make numerous permutations possible. The two routes selected give some of the best climbing and a look at the rest of the crag. Y Gelynen takes a line near the centre of the crag near an overhanging crack with two hollies, one in it and the second higher on the R., whilst Y Gilfach uses an obvious V-corner on the R. of the crag and on the R. of a green corner and three riblets. Many routes are possible up the quartz slabs on the L. of the cliff.

Start a little to the R. of the overhanging crack with the holly tree, below a V-chimney with a rowan tree below it.

1   50 ft.   Go direct to the rowan. (The V-chimney above gives the line of Dorcon an excellent VS.)

2   50 ft.   Follow the ledge L. and then get up onto the arête. Follow this to a stance and belay on a holly tree.

3   50 ft.   Get onto the rib on the L. to reach a stance below a wall.

4   50 ft.   Reach the overhang above by going R. and then L. Climb it and continue up the slab above to grass and a thread belay.

5   80 ft.   Go up the wall and then step round R. to finish with ease.

Taith Y Pererin (VD −) also climbs this stretch of rock keeping generally to the R. of this central fault.

187   Y Gilfach

S. 240 ft. * *Roberts, Dwyer, 1958.*

The R. side of Craig Yr Wrysgan is not so large as the central part but is quite steep. The large green corner has not been climbed but each of the ribs to

Plate 53. The crux of Mean Feet, missing out the stance. Asahel takes the slab in the L., bottom corner

the R. does give quite good climbing. The first is Space Beneath My Feet, HVS, with two slings for aid on the first groove and then a delightful arête. Romulus (VD) looks for difficulty up the central rib, whilst Babylon (VD) does the same on the R. hand one. However, Y Gilfach gives better climbing than those up the V-corner a few feet further R. A grassy approach or the lower part of either of the VD ribs bring one to the start.

1 30 ft.   Get up to the grass ledge at the foot of the corner.

2 60 ft.   Up the corner for 10 ft. and then out L. to a cave with thread belays.

3 60 ft.   Climb the steep slabs on the R. to a belay in the corner.

4 60 ft.   Climb the corner direct.

5 30 ft.   A short slab to the top.

188 Slack

S. 350 ft. * Cartledge, Lees, 1960.
Clogwyn Yr Oen (GR 673449) is best looked at from the mound opposite it on the other side of the road. A stone wall meets the toe of the buttress and this marks the division into two faces, the SW. face and the SE. face. Of the two routes described Kirkus' Climb Direct takes the dividing nose between the faces whilst Slack goes up the centre of the SE. face. Many other routes have been climbed and are possible. On the SW. face steep pockety walls give the lines of two VS's, Orange Outang which passes an obvious orange patch of rock and Pinky which takes the wall 30 ft. R. of this. On the SE. face one can discover easy variations to Kirkus' Climb, Chic (VD +) which lies 40 yds. R of Kirkus' starting up a rib, Slick (VD) up the large slab in the centre of the face and Bent (S −), which starts between Chic and Slick, but then moves R. to finish at a pinnacle on the R. However, 80 yds. from Kirkus' route can be found slabs leading up to a big pinnacle below and a little to the R. of a large overhang. Slack climbs these slabs and then turns the overhang on the L.

Start at the foot of the slabs.

1 80 ft.   Straight up, not without interest, to the pinnacle.

2 80 ft.   Climb the flake from the R. and then the

steep, hold covered wall above to a stance. Continue up a crack to a stance just below the overhangs.

3 60 ft. Go up to the overhangs (runner if rope drag is required) traverse L. to reach a rib running up past them and climb this (crux). Then R. to a good belay in a corner on the R.

4 80 ft. Climb the corner crack, strenuous, then another above and a simple section to a good grassy stance. Now either go easily to the top or walk across L. for 60 ft. to a delightful crack up a steep slab – this is the last pitch of Chic and is also a finish to Kirkus' Direct.

The best descent is by a gully on the L. of the crag.

189   Kirkus' Climb Direct

S. 290 ft. ** Kirkus bros. 1928.
Kirkus in fact did not climb all the pitches described but this combination is the best at the standard.

Start by the dry stone wall.

1 60 ft. Step from the wall onto the face and climb this and the slab above until a stance is reached. Continue up another slab just L. of an easy chimney until a stance in a sheltered nook of large blocks is reached.

2 80 ft. Bridge up the chimney until a long stride and a swing (well protected) lead out R. onto the edge. Now continue up the pocketed slab above, exposed, to reach a large grass ledge. Belay on the R.

3 90 ft. Get out L. onto the arête and follow a fine groove on good holds to a ledge. Walk R. a few ft. and make an interesting move onto the slabs above which lead easily to a good small stance and thread belay or nuts.

4 60 ft. Climb the groove above the belay and then easy slabs to a large mossy terrace.

It is now possible to scramble to the top of the crag, but a worthwhile excursion is to walk 40 ft. R. to the foot of a steep little corner and climb this (hard) to arrive at the foot of a steep slab split by a crack (the last pitch of Chic), and so finish up this (50 ft.).

190   Flake Wall

VS+ 140 ft. * Stewart, Kellett, 1955.
As one descends from Clogwyn Yr Oen, a small steep buttress can be seen about 100 yds. further over towards Llyn Stwlan. This is Clogwyn Y Bustach GR 672448) which gives the final route selected

in this area, and is well worth the extra few yds. walking.

Start below a large flake on the R. of the central nose of the crag.

1   70 ft.   Climb the flake by the groove and chimney on its L. Then step out L. onto the steep wall and move across below a shallow V-chimney. Move back up into the base of the chimney and then after one move up this, step out and climb its edge on fine holds to reach a small stance and nut belays at the top.

2   40 ft.   Follow a diagonal line of holds L. across the steep wall to a stance on the edge of the buttress.

3   30 ft.   Steep but much easier climbing to the top.

Crafnant. Craig Y Dwr and Clogwyn Yr Eryr

SE. Facing. 1,250 ft. above sea level. 200 ft. high, GR 732601 and 733605.

Many steep little cliffs can be found in this secluded valley which runs into the Carnedds from Trefriw. They can be reached by car to a last gate near the Mynydd Club hut at Blaen Y Nant (GR 738602). The crags are reached by a short walk up grass and scree from here.

Parking is not encouraged at the Mynydd hut so cars are best left just inside the last gate.

The nearest official rescue post is at Plas Y Brenin, Capel Curig. There is a phone box a little way down the road (GR 750609).

The routes described lie on two cliffs, Craig Y Dwr is the L. hand with a tree filled central gully and a fine clean top arête whilst Clogwyn Yr Eryr is the steep light coloured cliff at the top of the screes, very overhung at the base.

191   Vypon

VS+ 270 ft. Reeves and Williams, 1961.
Craig Y Dwr is a crag which a central tree filled gully breaks into two sections. S. Crag on the L. is basically composed of a long rib running up to a very steep final section, whilst the other half, N. Crag, has various short routes, particularly on the L. face with two wet weather climbs up the wall to the R. of centre. However, our route lies on the N. crag and

Plate 54. At the fifth peg. Connie's Crack

follows the most obvious features.

Start at the lowest point of the arête.

1   100 ft.   Scramble up the arête (avoiding the grass on either side!) with a harder move from a large flake to some trees.

2   80 ft.   Climb the steep arête for a few moves until a step R. leads to the foot of a crack. Climb this with a fine peg to a small ledge and then toe traverse very delicately R. to reach a corner. (If the leader has plenty of slack on this section, he could fall onto a bluebell covered ledge!) Climb the corner to a stance on a flake in an exposed position below the big roof.

3   60 ft.   Move R. to a chimney and with two or three pegs climb up to less steep slab on the L. and so to another small, exposed stance.

4   30 ft.   Get onto a ledge and then swing L. and use a poor peg to land on heather and top of crag.

192   Connie's Crack

A2/HVS− 160 ft. (7 pegs) ** **w** (*Clogwyn Yr Eryr*). *James, Lees, 1961.*

This crag is very steep and quite large. Most of the routes are good and in fact all the weaknesses on the crag have now been climbed. To the L. of centre are three grooves, the L. one undercut and an old threaded sling is the line of Clonus (ES− with 2 pegs), then after a line of overhangs is a narrower steep groove, Asteroth (HVS+ with 2 pegs) and then, less forbidding on the R. is Beelzebub (HVS).

Start under the overhangs between Clonus and Astoroth below a large square roof.

1   120 ft.   Climb strenuously up the pocketed arête on the L. of the niche to place a long ice peg in a hole in the L. wall of the niche above. Using this get into the niche and with two pegs get out of it to the groove above and L. Bridge up this for a few ft. (nut runners plus a hole on the R. arête) to a good nut sling usually in place. Use two pegs to traverse L. (**Plate 54**) and then climb free up the arête to a very small ledge. (Possible seat stance). Now climb the thin crack up the R. wall (2 pegs A1) until a swing can be made R. to reach steep free climbing which in 20 ft. leads to a large stance below a green groove (peg belays).

2   40 ft.   Bridge up the steep groove, finishing facing outward. Belay well back.

Ph   Pe

E Anglesey

Holyhead Mountain

All the good climbing on Anglesey is found on this mountain which rises over 700 ft. above sea level. A small crag can be found just below the summit facing sw. which gives some little practice climbs, but all the fierce climbing for which this area is renowned is found on the sea cliffs, which in places approach 400 ft. in height. Climbing on these cliffs is usually exceptionally steep, sometimes loose and often very serious, but the routes described here have been selected, not for their extreme difficulty but because they are popular and so have lost much of the loose rock and have become classics of this new style of climbing. Cliffs are found right round the seaward side of the mountain. Those on the N. coast are small and not often frequented, then from the Fog Signal Station at N. Stack they get bigger, including a fantastic roof, then a series of caves and zawns, the location of the final route in this book. Next comes a line of superb, gradually increasing cliffs called Craig Gogarth (**Plate 55**), which are now quite popular and give the majority of climbing described here. After this, a row of less attractive cliffs lead to the lighthouse at s. Stack. The final section of coast running SE. from s. Stack form a geologically fantastic series of zawns and walls culminating in a fine steep little wall, Castell Helen, which constitutes a fine introduction to the area.

No attempt will be made in this section to indicate hotels, guest houses, etc., as was done in the other areas, for those climbing on Anglesey are usually based in the conventional centres in the mountains and use the A5 road from Menai Bridge to reach the cliffs. From Holyhead follow the road past the docks and then along the sea front (Beach Road) until signposts lead inland to s. Stack. Follow these to a car park at a cafe (G R 208821) (Patrons only!) or a second car park 100 yds. further (G R 206822) just at the prow of the hill before the descent to the lighthouse (crowded in summer). Castell Helen lies just below the old tower seen from the first car park, whilst Mousetrap Zawn lies a few yds. below the second park and is bounded by the path to the light-

Plate 55. Craig Gogarth, main cliff

house from near which its route is well seen. Craig
Gogarth is reached from either park in about
15 mins. by walking roughly NE. across the moorland
on rough tracks until after passing a radio station
(avoid entry) and contouring round the landward
side a little hill and then cutting off the tracks by a
fainter path one reaches a grassy platform with fine
views of the crags. This is as far as some parties go
and still worth the walk!

Mountain rescue is difficult on these cliffs, needing
special equipment and skilled rescuers. In the event
of an accident on the major cliffs or in the zawns it is
best to use Holyhead Police to call out Ogwen
Cottage Mountain Rescue Team and also to arrange
a standby of R.A.F. Vally team if it is at all serious.
On matters of life or death, particularly when tides
are involved, helicopters can be used to ensure the
rapid arrival of rescuers and equipment.

193 Gogarth
HVS+ 380 ft. *** Ingle and Boyson, 1964.
Seen from the grass ledge at the arrival point, three
sections of crag are visible. In the distance rising
out of the sea in ever heightening walls is the main
crag. This terminates in a large (50 ft.) white pinnacle
which breaks the line of the sea-level traverse below
these cliffs. The cliffs between this pinnacle and the
descent gully are roughly divided into an upper and
lower section by a grass terrace. The lower section
rises from a sloping shelf in two grooves and a slab
whilst the upper section is more complex, starting on
the L. with slabs which blend with the main cliff and
which lead to an amphitheatre. These provide many
routes whilst the R. wall of the amphitheatre is made
up of a large slab which contain four fine routes. Then
comes a pinnacle, Shag Rock and finally between this
and the descent gullies a series of gullies, walls and
flakes, all giving routes of various standards. Three of
the routes selected lie on the main cliff, whilst two
others lie on the upper cliff and one on the lower.
Gogarth, the classic route of the crag, lies up the
white pinnacle and the walls directly above it.

Start by descending the gully and a steep path to
the boulder field at sea level, then ascending to
traverse the sloping slab below the lower cliff and
finally by a short descent to a big ledge below the
crack on the R. side of the pinnacle.

1   60 ft.   Climb the crack to a stance just below the top.

2   60 ft.   Cross the steep wall on the R. to a little slab below an overhang. Climb this until good holds lead L. to a slabby ledge. Take an uncomfortable peg belay in the middle of this.

3   70 ft.   Traverse to the L. end of the ledge and climb a steep groove with an awkward exit onto easier ground. Now go diagonally R. to finally mantel-shelf onto a fine 'bivouac' type ledge.

4   60 ft.   On the L. is a steep crack leading up to the top of a flake like pinnacle. Follow this, not too steep, to a stance at the top.

5   130 ft.   Again make a steep traverse R. across the wall, until a devious series of moves brings one suddenly to an old piton. Using this for protection and aid, move up to a very steep crack and jamb up into a shallow niche (crux). Finally follow the crack above, which alternates between being interesting and exciting, to the top.

194   Big Groove/Pentathol

ES—/HVS— 390 ft./340 ft. ** Crew and Alcock, 1966/ Crew and Alcock, 1964.

These two routes are described together because both have the same start, and one offers an escape if the other proves to be too hard. They lie half way along the main cliff about 100 yds. to the L. of Gogarth pinnacle.

Start by descending from the start of Gogarth and traversing L. round the pinnacle and under a very overhanging section of cliff (Dinosaur ES and Mammoth ES find ways up here) until a 4 ft. square block is nearly reached.

Start on a ledge about 10 ft. above the tide line near a short open V chimney.

1   120 ft.   Ignore the chimney and climb the wall R-wards on excellent holds except for one move, to reach a ledge below a short steep corner. Go up the corner for 10 ft. to reach a roof with thread runners and then move L. to reach an easier crack. Climb this until holds lead out L. to a good stance and low belays (possibly a piton).

2   40 ft.   For the Big Groove return to the corner and continue for a few ft. to a large ledge. Go from this to another good ledge below a great steep black corner – this is it! Peg belay.

Plate 56. At the crux of Phaedra

3 60 ft. Climb up the smooth wall on the L. to a spike and then struggle R. to find holds and a peg in the main groove. Climb this for a few ft. until an awkward move on the L. out of a slight recess (poor peg) brings one grasping onto a small stance. Peg belays.

4 100 ft. There is another groove on the L. which leads with less ferocity to a good stance.

5 70 ft. Delightfully easy climbing to the top.
or
2 40 ft. For Pentathol, climb the crack on the L. of the stance to reach large flake and so go easily L. to another good stance.

3 80 ft. Step L. to a rib which leads up into a steep groove, and climb this at about s. standard to below a steep overhang. Excellent protection. Now make a hard move over this to roll onto a slab, and so continue easily to another good stance.

4 100 ft. Walk up into the hollow behind and after a short wall and odd boulders escape to easy ground.

195 Phaedra

HVS— 150 ft. * Howells, Whybrow, 1966.
This fine route lies up the main cliff another 100 ft. along the traverse from Pentathol. Care with tides is needed on these routes.

Start at the foot of an overhanging chimney from which it is easily possible to scramble up a few ft. to a pillar on the arête on the L. below three grooves.

1 120 ft. Climb the central groove to the overhang (**Plate** *56*) and then move out L. (crux) at one of two levels until a good crack round the corner can be gained. Climb this until a mantel-shelf move L. on a spike in a very open position makes the continuation of the crack possible and leads to a good stance and spike belays.

2 30 ft. Continue up less steep rocks.

196 Simulator

VS. 120 ft. * Crew, Ingle, 1964.
The lower cliff is split by two grooves under which one passes to reach Gogarth (Route 193) and the main cliff routes. The R. groove gives Emulator (HVS) whilst the slabby wall on its R. is climbed by Imitator (vs+). However, the L. groove gives our route and this proves to be one of the most normal

on the crag, certainly giving the best introduction to the style of climbing.

Start below the groove.

1   120 ft.   Climb straight up to the bulge and go round this using lay away holds and the L. wall to reach a good resting ledge. A few steep moves up a thin crack in the L. wall lead to good holds and a shattered arête. Good belays are a long way back so 150 ft. of rope is useful.

197   Gauntlet

*HVS — . 220 ft. * Crew and Ingle, 1964.*

The L. half of the upper cliff is characteristically marked by a grey ramp on the L. (The Ramp, HVS) and a loose yellow groove on the R. This good climb takes a line just on the L. of the yellow groove which leads steeply at first to a more broken and open section in the upper half of the cliff.

Start 20 ft. L. of the yellow groove below a smooth groove.

1   80 ft.   Enter the groove and reach a peg with difficulty at 10 ft. Continue to below a bulge and climb this (crux). Now better holds lead R. over another overhang to a stance and peg belay.

2   70 ft.   First climb steeply up L. until a traverse R. and another cracked corner lead to a stance on the R.

3   70 ft.   Go L. and so take the crack steeply to the top. 30 ft. more to a belay.

198   Central Park

*HVS. 200 ft. **Crew and Alcock, 1966.*

The R. wall of the amphitheatre in the upper cliff is a huge slab marked by a crack (The Strand HVS +) on the L. and the pinnacle of Shag Rock on the R. Midway between these and in the upper section of the wall is an obvious crack which forms the top pitch of this route.

Start on the path directly below the final crack. Piton belay.

1   110 ft.   Step up a few ft. to the foot of a shallow groove. This can be awkward to start but soon leads to a line of good holds leading L. Follow these, usually firm (!), to the foot of a shallow v chimney. Make one move in this, then from a runner, traverse R. on smaller holds to a poor stance at the foot of the final crack.

Plate 57. At the peg on pitch 2 of Mousetrap

239

2   90 ft.   Climb the crack steeply on good holds until it narrows. Then make a hopeful swing up on jambs to reach a sloping ledge above and so via an open chimney reach grass stances, etc.

199   The Mousetrap

HVS— 420 ft. *** Brown and Crew, 1966.
The Mousetrap Zawn is the first bay on the coast s. of S. Stack. It is bounded on the L. by the zig-zag footpath down to the lighthouse and on the R. by a pinnacled and grassy arête which gives the usual descent route to the climb. The climb takes the wall of fantastically folded rock above the cave at the back of the zawn and gives tremendous climbing of a most unusual character.

Start from the second car park by crossing the wall at a gap and descend steepening grass to reach a pinnacle on a ledge. A long abseil should take one over rock, grass, and steep wet shelves to the boulder field in the zawn. Cross this to the far side of the cave below a groove of grey rock.

1   40 ft.   Step up into a subsidiary groove and after a few ft. in this move R. into the main groove and go up this to a stance with high peg belays.

2   110 ft.   Reach a peg in the wall on the R. with difficulty (**Plate 57**) and traverse across below this to a foothold in a chimney. Now swing out R. onto the overhanging rib and follow this to easier rock and a more broken chimney. Climb this moving R. where possible until a slab leads R. to a good stance.

3   70 ft.   Climb the steep wall on the R. to reach another characteristic chimney. Either follow this, delicate, with two pegs, or move further R. onto big creaky holds and use these. Either way reach the foot of an obvious ramp like slab. Follow this for 15 ft. to a stance.

4   80 ft.   Climb the slab, easily to a good stance and large belays.

5   120 ft.   Climb the niche behind the belay for a few moves and then swing out R. onto the steep red wall. Climb this moving R. at a bulge to a good ledge below a corner. Climb the corner direct with a peg at the top to reach ledges and a stance. (A harassed party could avoid the last 30 ft. by following a diagonal line L. up grass to easy ground

200   A Dream of White Horses

VS+ 370 ft. *** Ward-Drummond and Pearce, 1968.
This excellent and popular route lies on a great slab –
Web Slab – about a hundred yds. s. of N. Stack.
It is reached by parking near the disused quarries
on the N. coast at the end of the continuation of
Beach Road. From the end of the dirt road, a steep
rocky track leads along the cliff tops towards N.
Stack Fog Signal Station. Follow the track until it
splits just after its highest point, when a fainter path
on the L. leads to the R. hand of two shallow cols.
Cross this and descend steepening ground to arrive
on a flat headland with large boulders about
150 ft. above the sea. To the R., steep cliffs
continue with various caves towards N. Stack whilst
to the L. a superb zawn separates the headland from
the steep white rocks of Wen Slab. This route crosses
the Slab from R. to L. and is reached by scrambling
back round above the zawn and then down the R.
(s.) arête for about 150 ft. until once again you are
about 150 ft. above the sea. On a small ledge, good
spike belays can be found and a short open V
groove leads down gently onto the edge of the Slab.

1   20 ft.   Climb down the V groove to a sloping
stance with good chock belays.

2   150 ft.   Step down slightly and then traverse
across the slab past two good spikes. After about
40 ft. an old peg is reached. Step L. then up and so
in 20 more ft. to another peg. Step up L. and then
once more move up for a few ft. to regain the traverse
line and so reach good holds leading to a crack (Wen,
HVS−). Climb this crack (good spike runners) for
10 ft. until it is possible to either mantel-shelf or
step onto another raising traverse. Follow this
awkwardly to a small ledge. Various belays including
a large artificial hexagonal chock.

3   50 ft.   From the L. end of the stance, climb a
diagonal crack (hands in crack, feet on wall) to
reach a good spike. Traverse L. on good holds and
then step down to a poor stance (peg on L.).
Continue L. with an awkward step into an open
square chimney of poorish rock (Concrete Chimney
HVS). Two pegs for a belay.

4   120 ft.   Step up to reach a line of holds below
the overhangs and move across for a few ft. (peg?).
Now either move L. on undercut holds round a steep

nose or better (for the leader!) step down a few ft. until it is possible to move into an area of easier rock. Continue L. (runners and maybe a peg) round various noses until it is possible to step down onto a pleasant slab. Cross this to reach an open square chimney (peg). Move up this and finally out L. (rope drag!) to loose, grassy rocks and the top. Peg belays. Although this climb is not technically very hard, a fall by either leader or second on the final pitch could give problems. Seat harnesses seem sensible and adequate protection should be arranged however competent the party may appear.